HITLER AND NAZI GERMANY

HITLER AND
NAZI GERMANY

Edited by ROBERT G. L. WAITE
Williams College

HOLT, RINEHART AND WINSTON
New York   Chicago   San Francisco   Atlanta
Dallas   Montreal   Toronto   London   Sydney

CONTENTS

INTRODUCTION

Will anyone ever fully understand the monstrous experiences which befell us during the twelve years of the Third Reich?
—Friedrich Meinecke, *Die deutsche Katastrophe* (1946)

At first glance the problem of Adolf Hitler and the founding of Nazi Germany seems to be quite simple: here, apparently, is one more example of those "strong men on horseback" who—like Caesar and Napoleon—ride across the stage of history and establish authoritarian governments during periods of chaos and confusion. But in the case of Hitler this easy explanation will not do. Hitler did not look like a heroic leader; he looked like an apprentice waiter in a second-rate Viennese café; and although he was fascinated by horses, he was deathly afraid of them. More important, the Nazi dictatorship was not merely another form of authoritarian government. It was organized barbarism.[1] This government declared that there was no law except the will of the Führer; it institutionalized terror; it taught children to hate their neighbors and spy on their parents; it ordered the murder of millions of people whose only fault was that they were members of the "wrong" religion or political party or race; it burned great books of Western civilization and shouted with approval when one of its leaders said, "When I hear the word culture, I release the safety catch on my revolver." Nazism was not simply another type of authoritarianism; it was "the negation of God erected into a system of government."[2]

The problem of explaining German fascism is even more difficult when one recalls that this species of political and social cannibalism did not take place in a backward country a long time ago. It occurred in the twentieth century among one of the world's most advanced and literate people. How

[1] Hitler would have liked this characterization. Shortly after coming to power in 1933 he said, "They regard me as an uneducated barbarian. Yes, we are barbarians! We want to be barbarians! It is an honorable title." Quoted by Hermann Rauschning, *The Voice of Destruction* (New York, 1940), p. 80.

[2] William E. Gladstone used this phrase in his autobiography to characterize the government of the Two Sicilies under the notorious King Bomba [*Gleanings of Past Years* (New York, 1879), vol. IV, pp. 5-7].

1

was it possible that such a people accepted Hitler and gave him their over-whelming support? Will anyone indeed "ever fully understand these monstrous experiences?" It is the purpose of this book of readings to provide evidence and interpretations that will help students to understand one of the most baffling periods of all history.

Each of the three parts of this book examines one aspect of the Third Reich: Hitler's personality; reasons for the Nazi rise to power; the theory and practice of National Socialism.

Any study of Nazi Germany must center on Adolf Hitler, founder of the movement, then Führer and Chancellor of the Third Reich. Never in modern history has one man's personality so completely dominated and controlled a society. A brief interpretive sketch of Hitler's life introduces the first section. This essay also provides a survey of German history during the years of Hitler's domination. The next selection, drawn from Alan Bullock's standard biography, shows Hitler as a master of political opportunism and chicanery who was driven by personal ambition and lust for power. Bullock's discussion of Hitler's political techniques is a distinguished contribution, but it is not enough to conclude, as Bullock does, that Hitler was an evil man; nor is it enough simply to label him as an opportunist or a fanatic. He was clearly not a normal person, and it is useful to call upon psychiatrists to provide insight into his curious and compelling personality. Studies by such specialists help one to understand what kind of wicked man, what kind of opportunist, what sort of fanatic, he was.

Douglas M. Kelley, a psychiatrist, diagnoses Hitler as a compulsive neurotic with phobias that had a direct bearing on his success and his failure. Kelley's interest is in Hitler's personality as such; he is not concerned with his broad social and psychological background. In the next selection, written by the noted psychoanalyst and social psychologist Erich Fromm, the perspective is widened by showing the relationship between Hitler's personality and his appeal to the German people. Fromm maintains that this appeal was great, particularly among the lower middle class, precisely because these Germans shared Hitler's personality problems: they too possessed paranoic and sado-masochistic tendencies.

The second part is concerned with the difficult problem of historical causation. It asks the question that is at once the simplest and the most sophisticated the student can ask: What "caused" National Socialism? *Why* did it happen? Of the many answers historians have given to this question, four that stand out as particularly important are presented here. Even these major interpretations do not supply final answers. Rather, they lead to a continuing investigation and discussion of the complex and fascinating question of the causes of National Socialism. Authors of differing interpretations do not necessarily contradict each other. They may have used different evidence or placed a different emphasis on the same evidence. In what ways are the interpretations given here compatible? In what ways complementary? In what ways contradictory?

William L. Shirer, in his best-selling history of Nazi Germany, concludes that the Nazis came to power because their movement was "a logical continuation of German history."[3] This interpretation, which is shared by many other Western liberals, asserts that during the centuries prior to Hitler's accession to power in 1933 the "German character" was already displaying attitudes and ideas highly congenial to National Socialism. This school of thought maintains, for example, that for centuries leading German intellectuals had proclaimed the mystique of racism, endorsed the Leadership principle, extolled the power of the state, urged the submissiveness of the individual, scoffed at democracy, and worshiped the god of power. Protagonists of these ideas, it is alleged, are to be found in virtually every field: Luther in religion; Fichte, Hegel, and Nietzsche in philosophy; Kleist, Novalis, and Stefan George in literature; Treitschke, de Lagarde, and Spengler in history; Wagner in music. Prussia, this interpretation insists, had a particularly baneful effect on German history and made direct contributions to the Third Reich. In general, "Prussianism" pervaded all Germany; inculcated militarism, ruthless efficiency, and obsequiousness before authority; and stifled all humane and liberal tendencies. Bismarck, in particular, bequeathed a legacy of opposition to liberalism and the conviction that important political problems were to be resolved not by persuasion and appeal to opinion but by duplicity and the appeal to force. His dramatic successes, it is said, taught generations of Germans to distrust their own political judgment. Prussia also provided ruling classes inimical to democracy: the *Junkers,* the army, the industrialists, and the humorless, bristlingly efficient bureaucrats. Many historians of this school stress the importance of German militarism to the success of Hitler; others claim that he benefited enormously from the long history of German anti-Semitism.

Klaus Epstein takes serious exception to the thesis that Nazism was inherent in history. He asserts that Shirer distorts German history and misunderstands the complexities of twentieth-century totalitarianism, and he advises him to look for the causes of Nazism not in the long-distant past but in the specific social, economic, and political conditions existing in Germany during the months and years immediately preceding 1933. Whether these years contained the "causes" for the rise of Hitler or whether they served merely to accentuate tendencies that Shirer finds already in existence in German history is an open question.

The volatile British historian A. J. P. Taylor provides an impressive

---

[3] Other writers who have also concluded that the roots of Nazism are sunk deep in German history are cited in Suggestions for Additional Reading.

example of the political explanation for the advent of Hitler. He has no patience with those who urge the importance of intellectual history, or who generalize about the German character and sociopsychological factors, or who emphasize the role of Hitler's "demonic personality." Taylor's analysis is based on a close examination of German political life during the last years of the Weimar Republic: The political parties were atomized and ineffective; the political leadership, inexperienced and inept. But weak as they were, they could have stopped the "Bohemian corporal" if they had summoned the will to resist. Instead, they sought to accommodate him. Hitler's victory, according to this view, was the result of sordid political intrigue: he did not seize power; it was handed to him.

An economic explanation for the rise of Hitler is given next by Franz Neumann. Using a basically Marxian analysis, he concludes that Nazism was the inevitable consequence of the monopoly stage of capitalism. The Third Reich was the creation of powerful economic interests, notably the industrialists and the *Junker* landlords. These reactionary forces feared popular government and were convinced that they could use Hitler as a means of thwarting genuine social democracy. Consequently they entered into a conspiracy with the Nazi demagogues. Hitler was to attract and control the masses but the essentials of power were to be kept in the hands of the reactionary capitalists. Thus, to Neumann and the Marxist school, the theories advanced by the Nazis in an effort to justify their government were merely subterfuges for hoodwinking the masses and disguising the fact that actual power in Hitler's Germany did not lie with Hitler at all; it lay with the same forces that had controlled, in turn, the Empire, the Republic, and the Third Reich: the industrialists, the *Junkers,* the bureaucrats, and the army.

In the next selection, Zevedei Barbu, a social psychologist, introduces a new approach to the problem of causation. He finds the historical explanation of Shirer, the political emphasis of Taylor, and the economic interpretation of Neumann inadequate and unconvincing. Barbu asserts that we must seek answers in the psychological condition of the German people. The Nazis, he notes, recruited their members from a cross section of Germans, and Nazism both reflected and responded to their desires. Hitler succeeded not because of a conspiracy of the few but because his movement gave high hope to the many of solving the pressing psychological demands of a people living under conditions of acute stress. Defeated by war and broken by inflation, the uprooted, humiliated, and insecure Germans were attracted to Nazism because they felt that their personal problems would be solved by a movement that promised to supply everything they lacked as individuals: dramatic action, a sense of purpose, a feeling of power.

There are, of course, other interpretations of why Hitler came to power. Those of Gerhard Ritter and the late Friedrich Meinecke, two influential

German historians, are particularly worth noting. (See Suggestions for Additional Reading, p. 117.)

The last part of this book is devoted to discussions of Nazism in theory and practice. A careful consideration of the Third Reich in action is essential for two reasons: first, a historian's interpretation of *what* Nazism was like will inevitably influence his explanation of *why* or *how* Nazism came into being; second, any system of government must be evaluated not by its theoretical statements alone but by the results it produces. The questions here are these: What was the relationship between theory and practice in Hitler's Germany? What did Nazism mean in actual practice? What were the consequences of this system in both domestic and foreign affairs?

Alan Bullock introduces this section by setting forth the basic ideas of Adolf Hitler. Without denying the Führer's capacity for contrivance, Bullock insists that Hitler was really a man of theory—"an intellectual"—who held tenaciously to certain convictions which he put into practice during the Third Reich. The next two writers, Hannah Vogt and William Ebenstein, insist that never in human history have the practices of a government been so ruthlessly consistent with the theory. They show that Hitler's belief in crude social Darwinism and his commitment to racist anti-Semitism determined the education, economics, culture, and foreign policy—indeed the very life—of the Third Reich. In the name of those principles millions of helpless people were ruthlessly murdered. These writers assert that the real horror of Hitler was this: he meant what he said.

The relationship between theory and practice in Nazi economic policy is debated in the next two selections. In the first, Burton H. Klein concludes that Hitler's ideology had little effect on his economic practices. Klein contends that the Nazis did not force a huge rearmament program on Germany and did not prepare for a great war of conquest. On the contrary, the Nazi economy was fairly normal and operated according to accepted economic principles. For example, Hitler permitted only a modest rearmament program because he did not want either to incur large deficits or to cut down the flow of consumer goods. Prior to the actual outbreak of war in 1939, Klein concludes, Hitler's economy "produced both 'butter' and 'guns'—much more of the former and much less of the latter than has been commonly assumed." These conclusions are disputed by Wolfgang Sauer, one of the leading authorities on the government of the Third Reich. Sauer maintains that the economy was directly related to Hitler's theories about racial competition and warfare. He argues that from the outset of the regime, Hitler deliberately planned a great war of conquest; further, he rejected all principles of economics and established "an economy of plunder" which assumed that all economic difficulties could be solved only by aggressive war—a war that he was prepared to wage even if it precipitated a general European conflict.

A. J. P. Taylor's interpretation of Hitler and the causes of World War II differs markedly from Sauer's. Taylor insists that the Nazi leader was not a man of theory who planned to dominate the world. Indeed, he "did not make plans—for world conquest or for anything else." He was a cool-headed, adroit opportunist whose forte was his ability to wait and capitalize on the mistakes of others. He had come to power "for solidly democratic reasons"; he was a moderate statesman whose "foreign policy was that of his predecessors." All he really wanted, Taylor asserts, was to achieve "legitimate" German interests and revise the Versailles Treaty. Thus, in Taylor's view, appeasement was the best policy for the West; Neville Chamberlain—not Winston Churchill—was the wisest statesman of the interwar years; and the Munich Agreement was "the triumph of all that was best and most enlightened." Taylor's book has been hailed in the British *Observer* as "an almost flawless masterpiece," and a writer in the influential *New Statesman* compares him favorably with Macaulay and Gibbon. Certainly Taylor raises absolutely basic questions about the personality of Hitler and the character of Nazi Germany: What were Adolf Hitler's plans and ambitions? Was he, as Taylor says, an adroit opportunist who deceived both his contemporaries and later historians? Was he a scheming power-hungry tyrant (Bullock)? Or was he a man dedicated to certain fixed ideas and driven by demons and a twisted psyche (Fromm, Kelley)? Did the Nazis have only limited objectives in foreign policy or did they consciously organize their entire society for the purposes of waging aggressive war?

The last selection is written by H. R. Trevor-Roper, Taylor's most constant and least charitable critic. In addition to providing a sustained and slashing attack on Taylor's interpretations, Trevor-Roper's essay serves as a résumé of the problems presented in this book of readings: Which interpretation of Hitler's personality and purposes is the most valid? What forces brought Hitler to power? Finally, what conclusions can be reached about Nazi Germany? Was it the product of expediency or the consequence of commitment? Did Hitler and the Nazis deliberately maneuver to bring about events or were events forced upon them? Were they fanatics who, in some way, were impelled to totalitarianism, genocide, and war?

"History," Pieter Geyl, a perceptive Dutch historian, has said, "is argument without end." And so it is. But the arguments historians use are of unequal value; some interpretations are better than others. Each student must reach his own conclusions, basing them on a careful and honest evaluation of the evidence and a critical appraisal of the conclusions reached by others. In this sense, Everyman is indeed his own historian.

In the reprinted selections footnotes appearing in the original sources have in general been omitted unless they contribute to the argument or better understanding of the selection.

This essay is designed to serve as an introduction to Hitler's life and personality and as a brief overview of German history during the Third Reich. In addition to noting the factual data given here about Hitler and his Reich, observe that this interpretation differs markedly from those in other selections. ROBERT G. L. WAITE (1919–   ) is the author of a study dealing with the postwar origins of National Socialism, *Vanguard of Nazism: The Free Corps Movement in Postwar Germany* (Cambridge, Mass., 1952) and co-translator of Erich Eyck, *A History of the Weimar Republic*, 2 vols. (Cambridge, Mass., 1962-63.)*

Adolf Hitler: A Life Sketch

Adolf Hitler, dictator of Nazi Germany from 1933 until his suicide in 1945, was the most powerful ruler of the modern era. It was he who set the standards for German art, medicine, music, and literature. He established educational and economic policies. He determined the foreign policy of the nation, and at his command thousands of young soldiers died in hopeless battle—many with the name of the Führer on their lips. His will became the law of the land. On his orders millions of innocent people were tortured, maimed, and murdered. For over a decade he was the arbiter of the fate of nations and the peace of the world. This bizarre little man, who looked so commonplace and vulnerable but who strode Europe like a colossus, was never graduated from high school and had never held a responsible position in military or civil life. By his forties, on the eve of becoming Chancellor, he seemed a failure in all his undertakings.

He was born of humble parents in an Austrian village inn on April 20, 1889. His own family genealogy could never have satisfied the racial laws he later imposed upon others. Of his father's parentage, it is clear only that he was born out of wedlock to one Marianne Schickelgruber, a servant girl who had worked in Graz—possibly in a Jewish household. Certainly Hitler was later haunted by a suspicion which to him was horrendous: that he himself might be "tainted" with Jewish blood. As dictator he ordered his secret police on three different occasions to investigate his par-

* Adapted from Robert G. L. Waite's essay on Hitler in *Collier's Encyclopedia* (1963 edition). Used by permission of The Crowell-Collier Publishing Company.

ents' racial background, but no definite conclusions were reached.

The most striking thing about Hitler's childhood is that it lasted until his death. He had no capacity for intellectual, emotional, artistic, or sexual development. As a boy he read books to confirm his own prejudices; and he continued to do so throughout his life. As a child he was subject to violent temper tantrums; as Führer he was famous for them. The musical and literary tastes of both the child and chancellor remained the same: Wagnerian opera, and stories about German gods and American cowboys. The Führer's favorite movie was *King Kong*. As a boy Hitler loved to eat pastry, go on picnics, stare at pretty girls, stay up late at night, and talk; in later years these habits were intensified. The political prejudices of his adolescence became, as we shall see, the political program of the German dictator. Indeed the sheer constancy of his thought and his inability to modify or change his basic ideas remained the most characteristic qualities of his mind. Opportunistic and flexible in many other areas, he did not alter his beliefs and prejudices. The ideas that attracted him as an adolescent formed the basis for the political program of the street agitator and the gist of the dying Führer's last will and testament. Throughout his life his ideas remained substantially unchanged, as did the words and phrases in which he expressed them. Moreover, the same mistakes in spelling and grammar appear in his post cards written as a boy from Vienna, his letters from the Front during World War I, and his notes decades later as Chancellor of Germany.

Adolf spent his boyhood in lovely villages of Upper Austria and in Linz, the provincial capital. Having failed to do passing work in the *Realschulen* of both Linz and Steyr, he feigned illness in 1905 and his widowed mother, who indulged his every whim, permitted him to quit school. He became something of a dandy, affecting black kid gloves, a derby hat, and an ivory-handled mahogany walking stick, and he scornfully rejected suggestions that he work to help defray his mother's expenses as beneath his dignity. His time was spent attending the local theater and opera, copying romantic paintings, reading tawdry adventure stories, and communing with the spirits of Teutonic heroes in the forests and castle ruins that surround Linz. His only friend in these years was August Kubizek, an upholsterer's son, who served as audience for his impassioned orations. To him the future Führer raged against the bourgeois world; to him he spoke of rebuilding cities and nations and outlined his plans for creating a greater, racially pure German *Reich*.

In September 1907 Hitler left Linz and his mother, who was dying of cancer, and went to Vienna to study art. Rejected by the academies of art and of architecture, he nevertheless kept up the pretense that he was an art student in order to continue receiving half of the orphan's allotment which would otherwise have gone to relatives who were struggling to bring up his younger sister. When at the age of twenty-two he was forced by court order to relinquish the pension, he made a precarious living by painting and selling post cards and drawing advertisements for boots and soap flakes. There is no evidence that he ever painted a house, hung wallpaper, or worked as a manual laborer. There is evidence, however, that he persuaded a crippled aunt, who had worked as a charwoman, to make him a large gift of money and to leave him the bulk of her life's savings. Her money enabled him to live in comfort in a home for men and to spend his afternoons reading extremist political pamphlets and his evenings orating against the ills of society or attending Wagnerian opera.

Hitler later considered that these years in Vienna (1907-1913) provided the most important educational experience of his life. All he had to do later, he wrote, was "add a few details" to the "great ideas" he had acquired during this period.

The ideas came largely from the writings of racist pamphleteers, notably Lanz von Liebenfels, whose theory of *Theozoologie* divided all people into two groups: Aryan supermen and animal subhumans, the most evil of whom were the Jews. Lanz preached a crude sort of social Darwinism and proclaimed that a struggle to the death between the two antagonists was inevitable. The superior "pure-souled" Aryans would ultimately prevail, but only if they chose a great Leader who would acquire an expanded *Lebensraum* (living space) in the East, establish a racially pure state, and prepare for the coming struggle. The symbol of the new *Reich* would be the *Hakenkreuz* (swastika); the sign of the "Holy Knighthood" of the blond elite within the *Reich* would be the runic letters ⚡⚡—symbols Hitler later adopted for his elite Black Shirts. In the new state, the racially unacceptable would be sterilized, used as slave laborers, or exterminated. Once this expanded, purified, and militarized state was established, Lanz prophesied, the Führer would launch the climactic world struggle against the "hydra-headed enemy led by international Jewry." Hitler put all these incredible fantasies of his youth into practice thirty-five years later in the slave-labor battalions and death camps of the Third Reich.

On May 24, 1913, Hitler, who had repeatedly failed to report for military training, fled Vienna to escape arrest as a draft dodger from the Austrian army. He lived in Munich until the outbreak of World War I, when he volunteered for service in the German army. During the war he served as a dispatch runner on the Western Front. He was promoted to corporal, was wounded twice, and was awarded the Iron Cross, both First and Second Class, for conspicuous bravery.

After the armistice, Hitler returned to Munich, where he met racist agitators who confirmed his childhood beliefs. His hatred for Jews became intensified, as did his obsession with building a racially pure state. He enlisted in the espionage section of an army regiment, and was assigned to spy on political parties. On September 12, 1919, he investigated the German Workers' Party—one of the many nationalist, racist groups that mushroomed in Munich in the postwar years—and joined it. He had finally found in this small party an outlet for his talents in political agitation and party organization. During the next two years he changed the name of the party to National Socialist German Workers' Party (*Nationalsozialistiche Deutsche Arbeiterpartei*), which was abbreviated NSDAP or Nazi Party (for the first two syllables).

The party espoused essentially the ideas Hitler had become addicted to in Vienna: violent racial nationalism, anti-Semitism, opposition to liberal democracy, and the "Leadership and Followship" principle. Just as he took his ideas from others, so the party adopted the symbols and organization of other groups: the swastika and the *Heil* greeting were taken from older German racist groups; the "German salute" and the use of Storm Troops (SA, from

Sturm Abteilung) to smash opposition meetings, from Italian Fascism.

The year 1923 seemed to give Hitler the opportunity to fulfill his frequent promise to "march on Berlin" and overthrow the government of "Jewish-Marxist traitors." In careful preparation he had made the acquaintance of General Erich Ludendorff, an old man, bitter and reactionary, but one whose name still carried prestige and whom Hitler saw as a useful front for his revolutionary activities. He and Ludendorff proclaimed the "National Revolution" on the night of November 8, 1923, in the Bürgerbräukeller in Munich. The next day they and other Nazi leaders marched on the War Ministry, but their road to it was blocked by a cordon of police. The police fired on the column of marchers and dispersed them. Hitler ran away.

Later arrested and brought to trial for high treason, he converted the proceedings into a propaganda triumph in which he "indicted" the president of the republic for treason and swore that one day he would bring his accusers into his own court. Although sentenced to five years' imprisonment in Landsberg, he served less than one year. During his confinement, he ate breakfast in bed, walked in the garden, lectured his fellow prisoners, and drew cartoons for a prison newspaper. He also dictated the first volume of his political observations, calling it "Four and a Half Years of Struggle Against Lies, Stupidity, and Cowardice." Later published under the title *Mein Kampf* (My Struggle), the book sold some ten million copies and made Hitler a wealthy man.

After his release from prison in December, 1924, Hitler went to the Obersalzberg, the mountains above the village of Berchtesgaden, where he lived in various inns for several years and in 1928 rented a villa, which he later bought, rebuilt, and named the Berghof. This mountain retreat was the locale not only of his periods of relaxation but also of many significant diplomatic meetings, including meetings with Neville Chamberlain of England and Kurt von Schuschnigg of Austria.

During these years he revised his tactics and decided to take the "legal way" to power. He reorganized the Nazi Party and engaged in an intensive campaign for votes. In the course of one speechmaking tour, he spoke in twenty-one cities in seven days. As he had promised in *Mein Kampf*, the Nazi meetings were cleverly planned mass meetings which combined some of the emotional attractions of American football rallies, evangelical prayer meetings, and Wagnerian opera. His speeches were designed to appeal to the emotions, not to the intelligence, of his audiences, and they repeated the same simple themes: avenge Versailles, crush the "traitors of the Weimar Republic," smash the Jews and Communists, and make the fatherland triumphant over all its enemies.

In the economic crisis and political confusion of the years 1930–1933, Hitler's impassioned promises attracted members of all social groups in Germany, but he made particular headway among the veterans of World War I and the lower middle class, for these groups felt acutely the humiliation of defeat, the threat of communism, the dread of unemployment, and the need for a powerful leader. In this same period Hitler began to reach the industrial leaders of Germany and convince them that his plans would redound to their benefit. High-ranking army leaders, too, were persuaded that the military figured largely in his scheme of German nationalism. Another important source of support was the *Landbund,* or League of Land Owners, which bitterly opposed the Weimar Republic's proposal to redistribute land and end the agricultural quota system which benefited the large farmers.

Hitler's actual "seizure of power" was made possible by a political deal he made with former Chancellor Franz von Papen. The two met on January 4, 1933, in greatest secrecy and agreed to work together for a government in which Hitler would be chancellor and von Papen's supporters would hold important ministries, and they agreed to the elimination of Social Democrats, Communists, and Jews from leading positions. Von Papen's support also brought the Nazi Party substantial financial support from German business circles. On January 30, 1933, the "Bohemian corporal" swore to defend the constitution of the Weimar Republic and, placing his soft, effeminate hands between the gnarled old palms of the senile president, Field Marshall von Hindenberg, in the ancient gesture of homage, became Chancellor of the Weimar Republic. With the death of Hindenberg a year later Hitler took the dual title "Führer and Chancellor" of Germany. The first title stressed Hitler's emphasis on his role of Leader of the new Nazi *Weltanschauung* (outlook on life). The second emphasized his claim to be the legal head of the German government. Both the general public and his closest associates addressed him as *"Mein Führer."*

The new ruler of Germany was a man of contrasts. As his war record testifies, he possessed great personal courage, yet he was haunted by petty fears: he was afraid of sunshine, horses, snow, and water. He was one of the most effective orators of history who through the spoken word excited crowds to the point of hysteria; in private conversation he was a bore. He was a hard-headed rationalist, a master of practical political

organization and technique, an expert on armament so knowledgeable that he impressed generals and admirals; he was also a superstitious fanatic driven by obsessions. He despised religion, but he announced on one occasion that he was the instrument of God and on another he said, "I go the way that Providence dictates with all the assurance of a sleepwalker." Socially he felt insecure and timid: he worried about wearing the correct tie; when he was host, he nervously checked and rechecked the arrangements, constantly seeking reassurance that his guests would have a good time. He was also arrogant, boorish, and insufferably rude. He had to dominate every conversation and would never admit a mistake. The man who demanded selfless patriotism of others announced in 1945, "The German people are not worthy of me. Let them perish." His personal magnetism is attested to by everyone who met him, yet the Führer was friendless. He murdered the one man who had ever called him by his first name.

Hitler moved rapidly to consolidate his power and establish his "thousand-year Reich." During his first months as head of the government he outlawed all other political parties, appointed Nazis as state governors, dissolved the trade unions, and organized men, women, and children into party-controlled groups. One of his major concerns was to alert the country to the perils of the "Red terror" in order to cement his own position. On the night of February 27, 1933, the Reichstag was set afire. The Nazis immediately laid the arson to a Communist plot and in the ensuing elections profited greatly from the trumped-up charge.

By the summer of 1934, Hitler met serious opposition within his own party. Dissatisfaction and dissension centered around the SA and its leader Captain Ernest Röhm. The "Old Fighters" of the SA demanded more radical social reforms, calling for "a second revolution," and they insisted on playing a larger role in the army. The German generals opposed the radicalism and military pretensions of the SA and told Hitler that the army would not continue to support him unless he thwarted the ambitions of the Storm Troops. Hitler, needing the approval of the army and suspicious of the restless SA, turned against his former friends. Professing to believe that Röhm planned "to eliminate me personally," he directed the so-called "Blood Purge" of June 30, 1934. The murder of Röhm and some hundred and fifty SA leaders, was followed by the death of hundreds of others whom Hitler considered possible threats to his dictatorship. When the army and the judiciary passively accepted these murders, the rule of law had ended in Germany. Shortly afterward army officers swore an oath of absolute allegiance not to the constitution or to the country but to Hitler. The highest judge in Germany announced that "the law and the constitution are the will of our Führer."

Hitler's final purpose went beyond legal, political, and social control. "Our revolution will never be complete," he once observed, "until we have dehumanized human beings." In his attempt to achieve this goal, he ordered the schools to teach brutality and hatred; he established a secret police (the *Gestapo*) to spy on the German people, concentration camps to break their will, and a "Ministry of Propaganda and Enlightment" to reshape their thinking. The Jews, whom he still considered the archenemies of mankind, were deprived of all civil rights, publicly humiliated, and finally murdered by the millions in a calculated attempt to destroy the entire Jewish people.

As soon as the German parliament had given him dictatorial powers, Hitler began to prepare for the war of aggression and revenge he had promised his boyhood companion August Kubizek and the readers of *Mein Kampf*. He re-established universal military service, built a powerful air force (under the guise of advancing civil aviation), and also in other ways violated the disarmament clauses of the Treaty of Versailles. In 1936 he occupied and fortified the Rhineland and repudiated the Locarno Pact. Insatiable in his lust for power and *Lebensraum*, he kept Europe in turmoil. Austria was forced into *Anschluss* (political union) with Germany, and on March 14, 1938, Hitler made a triumphal entry into Vienna. On September 29, 1938, he and Mussolini met at Munich with Prime Minister Chamberlain of England and Premier Daladier of France, who agreed to the surrender of the Sudetenland by Czechoslovakia. By the middle of October German troops had occupied the area, and Hitler prepared for the next "crisis." On March 15, 1939, German troops entered Prague, and the absorption of Czechoslovakia was complete. In August 1939, with considerable cynicism on both sides, Germany and the Soviet Union signed a nonaggression pact that freed Hitler in the East and enabled him to turn his full attention to the destruction of Europe.

On September 1, 1939, Hitler launched the attack against Poland that started World War II. He took personal command of the armed forces and pushed his plans for total war against the strong conviction of army leaders—particularly General Ludwig Beck, chief of the army general staff—that Germany was not yet strong enough to defeat the Western powers. As the war progressed and

Britain refused to come to terms, despite the successive collapse of Denmark, Norway, Holland, Belgium, and finally France, Hitler somewhat hesitantly decided on invasion of England. The overwhelming difficulties of such an operation were continuously stressed by both army and navy leaders, however, and Germany's massive air attacks failed—inexplicably to Hitler—to bring Britain to its knees. In October 1940 he issued a directive canceling Operation Sea Lion, code name for the invasion. Nevertheless, the series of decisive victories that had made him master of Europe convinced him that his "infallible intuition" had proved him to be "the greatest military commander of all time."

The determination to conquer Russia was never long out of Hitler's mind—indeed, it was plainly stated in *Mein Kampf*, as were so many of his plans which took the world by surprise when he began to implement them. On June 22, 1941, he invaded Russia. Neither his "infallible intuition" nor his "iron will" nor the squandered bravery of his troops was sufficient to prevail. The German attack faltered, stopped, was driven back.

Meanwhile, on July 20, 1944, the last of several attempts to assassinate Hitler took place when a time bomb was exploded in his field headquarters. His narrow escape convinced him that he had been chosen by God to lead the German people and that the nation would never fall as long as he was in Berlin. As British and American forces advanced from the west and their Russian allies moved in from the east, Hitler cowered in his Berlin air raid shelter, refusing to visit the front or to look at the bombed-out cities of Germany. He received enormous injections of vitamins, sedatives, stimulants, and hormones which Theodor Morell, his quack doctor, prescribed for *paralysis agitans*, a progressive nervous disease with which he may have been afflicted. He ordered nonexistent armies to attack, dispatched twelve-year-old boys to defeat the encircling enemy, ate pastry by the platterful, and talked interminably about the art of the Incas, the training of dogs, and the benefits of a vegetarian diet. On April 15, 1945, he was joined in the shelter by Eva Braun, his female companion for more than twelve years. Throughout his days of power he had sought—with considerable success—to keep their affair from public knowledge. As he neared the end, however, he permitted her to be with him, and in the early morning hours of April 29 they were married. This accomplished, Hitler drew up his will and testament to the German people, in which he blamed the war on "the poisoner of all peoples, international Jewry."

The end was a fitting climax to so gross and monstrous a career. At about 3:30 on the afternoon of April 30, 1945, Adolf Hitler swallowed a lethal dose of cyanide. As his face contorted and turned blue, his bride shot him through the left temple with her Walther 6.35 pistol. She then poisoned herself. Their bodies were dumped into a trough near a cement mixer, doused with 220 litres of petrol and ignited. The charred remains were found four days later by Russian soldiers. Identification was made by a careful examination of Hitler's rotting teeth.

ALAN BULLOCK (1914-   ) is Master of St.
Catherine's College, Oxford, and a leading authority
on Nazi German history. His recently revised
biography of Hitler is considered the most
authoritative work on the subject and, indeed, the
best single book yet written dealing with the
Third Reich. In the selection reprinted here Bullock
concludes that the rise and fall of Nazi Germany
were due primarily to Hitler's strengths and
weaknesses as a political leader. What aspects of
Hitler's personality and political techniques made
him an effective dictator?*

The Führer: Portrait of a Dictator

In the spring of 1938, on the eve of his greatest triumphs, Adolf Hitler entered his fiftieth year. His physical appearance was unimpressive, his bearing still awkward. The falling lock of hair and the smudge of his moustache added nothing to a coarse and curiously undistinguished face, in which the eyes alone attracted attention. In appearance at least Hitler could claim to be a man of the people, a plebian through and through, with none of the physical characteristics of the racial superiority he was always invoking. The quality which his face possessed was that of mobility, an ability to express the most rapidly changing moods, at one moment smiling and charming, at another cold and imperious, cynical and sarcastic, or swollen and livid with rage.

Speech was the essential medium of his power, not only over his audiences but over his own temperament. Hitler talked incessantly, often using words less to communicate his thoughts than to release the hidden spring of his own and others' emotions, whipping himself and his audience into anger or exaltation by the sound of his voice. Talk had another function, too. 'Words,' he once said, 'build bridges into unexplored regions.' As he talked, conviction would grow until certainty came and the problem was solved.

Hitler always showed a distrust of argument and criticism. Unable to argue

* Pages 372–382, 384–385, *Hitler: A Study in Tyranny.* Completely revised edition by Alan Bullock. Copyright © 1962 by Alan Bullock. Reprinted by permission of Harper & Row, Publishers, Incorporated, and Odhams Press Limited, with some of the footnotes omitted.

coolly himself, since his early days in Vienna his one resort had been to shout his opponent down. The questioning of his assumptions or of his facts rattled him and threw him out of his stride, less because of any intellectual inferiority than because words, and even facts, were to him not a means of rational communication and logical analysis, but devices for manipulating emotion. The introduction of intellectual processes of criticism and analysis marked the intrusion of hostile elements which disturbed the exercise of this power. . . .

As an orator Hitler had obvious faults. The timbre of his voice was harsh, very different from the beautiful quality of Goebbel's. He spoke at too great length; was often repetitive and verbose; lacked lucidity and frequently lost himself in cloudy phrases. These shortcomings, however, mattered little beside the extraordinary impression of force, the immediacy of passion, the intensity of hatred, fury, and menace conveyed by the sound of the voice alone without regard to what he said.

One of the secrets of his mastery over a great audience was his instinctive sensitivity to the mood of a crowd, a flair for divining the hidden passions, resentments and longings in their minds. In *Mein Kampf* he says of the orator: 'He will always follow the lead of the great mass in such a way that from the living emotion of his hearers the apt word which he needs will be suggested to him and in its turn this will go straight to the hearts of his hearers.'

One of his most bitter critics, Otto Strasser, wrote:

I have been asked many times what is the secret of Hitler's extraordinary power as a speaker. I can only attribute it to his uncanny intuition, which infallibly diagnoses the ills from which his audience is suffering. . . . Adolph Hitler enters a hall. He sniffs the air. For a minute he gropes, feels his way, senses the atmosphere. Suddenly he bursts forth. His words go like an arrow to their target, he touches each private wound on the raw, liberating the mass unconscious, expressing its innermost aspirations, telling it what it most wants to hear.

. . . The conversations recorded by Hermann Rauschning for the period 1932–4, and by the table talk at the Führer's H.Q. for the period 1941–2, reveal Hitler in another favourite role, that of visionary and prophet. This was the mood in which Hitler indulged, talking far into the night, in his house on the Obersalzberg, surrounded by the remote peaks and silent forests of the Bavarian Alps; or in the Eyrie he had built six thousand feet up on the Kehlstein, above the Berghof, approached only by a mountain road blasted through the rock and a lift guarded by doors of bronze. There he would elaborate his fabulous schemes for a vast empire embracing the Eurasian Heartland of the geopoliticians; his plans for breeding a new élite biologically preselected; his design for reducing whole nations to slavery in the foundation of his new empire. Such dreams had fascinated Hitler since he wrote *Mein Kampf*. It was easy in the late 1920s and early 1930s to dismiss them as the product of a disordered and overheated imagination soaked in the political romanticism of Wagner and Houston Stewart Chamberlain. But these were still the themes of Hitler's table talk in 1941–2 and by then, master of the greater part of Europe and on the eve (as he believed) of conquering Russia and the Ukraine, Hitler had shown that he was capable of translating his fantasies into a terrible reality. The invasion of Russia, the S.S. extermination squads, the planned elimination of the Jewish race; the treatment of the Poles and Russians, the Slav *Untermenschen*—these, too, were the fruits of Hilter's imagination.

All this combines to create a picture of which the best description is Hitler's own famous sentence: 'I go the way that Providence dictates with the assurance of a sleepwalker.' The former French Ambassador speaks of him as 'a man possessed'; Hermann Rauschning writes: 'Dosteovsky might well have invented him, with the morbid derangement and the pseudo-creativeness of his hysteria'; one of the Defence Counsel at the Nuremberg Trials, Dr. Dix, quoted a passage from Goethe's *Dichtung und Wahrheit* describing the Demoniac and applied this very aptly to Hitler. With Hitler, indeed, one is uncomfortably aware of never being far from the realm of the irrational.

But this is only half the truth about Hitler, for the baffling problem about this strange figure is to determine the degree to which he was swept along by a genuine belief in his own inspiration and the degree to which he deliberately exploited the irrational side of human nature, both in himself and others, with a shrewd calculation. For it is salutary to recall, before accepting the Hitler Myth at anything like its face value, that it was Hitler who invented the myth, assiduously cultivating and manipulating it for his own ends. So long as he did this he was brilliantly successful; it was when he began to believe in his own magic, and accept the myth of himself as true, that his flair faltered.

So much as been made of the charismatic [1] nature of Hitler's leadership that it is easy to forget the astute and cynical politician in him. It is this mixture of calculation and fanaticism, with the dif-

[1]The word is used by Max Weber to describe the authority of those who claim to be divinely inspired and endowed by Providence with a special mission.

ficulty of telling where one ends and the other begins, which is the peculiar characteristic of Hitler's personality: to ignore or underestimate either element is to present a distorted picture....

One of Hitler's most habitual devices was to place himself on the defensive, to accuse those who opposed or obstructed him of aggression and malice, and to pass rapidly from a tone of outraged innocence to the full thunders of moral indignation. It was always the other side who were to blame, and in turn he denounced the Communists, the Jews, the Republican Government, or the Czechs, the Poles, and the Bolsheviks for their 'intolerable' behaviour which forced him to take drastic action in self-defence.

Hitler in a rage appeared to lose all control of himself. His face became mottled and swollen with fury, he screamed at the top of his voice, spitting out a stream of abuse, waving his arms wildly and drumming on the table or the wall with his fists. As suddenly as he had begun he would stop, smooth down his hair, straighten his collar and resume a more normal voice.

This skilful and deliberate exploitation of his own temperament extended to other moods than anger. When he wanted to persuade or win someone over he could display great charm. Until the last days of his life he retained an uncanny gift of personal magnetism which defies analysis, but which many who met him have described. This was connected with the curious power of his eyes, which are persistently said to have had some sort of hypnotic quality. Similarly, when he wanted to frighten or shock, he showed himself a master of brutal and threatening language, as in the celebrated interviews with Schuschnigg and President Hacha.

Yet another variation in his roles was

the impression of concentrated will-power and intelligence, the leader in complete command of the situation and with a knowledge of the facts which dazzled the generals or ministers summoned to receive his orders. To sustain this part he drew on his remarkable memory, which enabled him to reel off complicated orders of battle, technical specifications and long lists of names and dates without a moment's hesitation. Hitler cultivated this gift of memory assiduously. The fact that subsequently the details and figures which he cited were often found to contain inaccuracies did not matter: it was the immediate effect at which he aimed. The swiftness of the transition from one mood to another was startling: one moment his eyes would be filled with tears and pleading, the next blazing with fury, or glazed with the faraway look of the visionary. Hitler, in fact, was a consummate actor, with the actor's and orator's facility for absorbing himself in a role and convincing himself of the truth of what he was saying at the time he said it. In his early years he was often awkward and unconvincing, but with practice the part became second nature to him, and with the immense prestige of success behind him, and the resources of a powerful state at his command, there were few who could resist the impression of the piercing eyes, the Napoleonic pose, and the 'historic' personality.

Hitler had the gift of all great politicians for grasping the possibilities of a situation more swiftly than his opponents. He saw, as no other politician did, how to play on the grievances and resentments of the German people, as later he was to play on French and British fear of war and fear of Communism. His insistence upon preserving the forms of legality in the struggle for power

showed a brilliant understanding of the way to disarm opposition, just as the way in which he undermined the independence of the German Army showed his grasp of the weaknesses of the German Officer Corps.

A German word, *Fingerspitzengefühl*—'finger-tip feeling'—which was often applied to Hitler, well describes his sense of opportunity and timing.

No matter what you attempt [Hitler told Rauschning on one occasion], if an idea is not yet mature you will not be able to realize it. Then there is only one thing to do: have patience, wait, try again, wait again. In the subconscious, the work goes on. It matures, sometimes it dies. Unless I have the inner, incorruptible conviction: *This is the solution,* I do nothing. Not even if the whole Party tries to drive me into action.

Hitler knew how to wait in 1932, when his insistence on holding out until he could secure the Chancellorship appeared to court disaster. Foreign policy provides another instance. In 1939 he showed great patience while waiting for the situation to develop after direct negotiations with Poland had broken down and while the Western Powers were seeking to reach a settlement with Soviet Russia. Clear enough about his objectives, he contrived to keep his plans flexible. In the case of the annexation of Austria and of the occupation of Prague, he made the final decision on the spur of the moment.

Until he was convinced that the right moment had come Hitler would find a hundred excuses for procrastination. His hesitation in such cases was notorious: his refusal to make up his mind to stand as a Presidential candidate in 1932, and his attempt to defer taking action against Röhm and the S.A. in 1934, are two obvious examples. Once he had made up his mind to move, however, he would act boldly, taking considerable risks, as in the reoccupation of the Rhineland in 1936, or the invasion of Norway and Denmark just before the major campaign in the west. . . .

No régime in history has ever paid such careful attention to psychological factors in politics. Hitler was a master of mass emotion. To attend one of his big meetings was to go through an emotional experience, not to listen to an argument or a programme. Yet nothing was left to chance on these occasions. Every device for heightening the emotional intensity, every trick of the theatre was used. The Nuremberg rallies held every year in September were masterpieces of theatrical art, with the most carefully devised effects. 'I had spent six years in St Petersburg before the war in the best days of the old Russian ballet,' wrote Sir Nevile Henderson, 'but for grandiose beauty I have never seen a ballet to compare with it.' To see the films of the Nuremberg rallies even today is to be recaptured by the hypnotic effect of thousands of men marching in perfect order, the music of the massed bands, the forest of standards and flags, the vast perspectives of the stadium, the smoking torches, the dome of searchlights. The sense of power, of force and unity was irresistible, and all converged with a mounting crescendo of excitement on the supreme moment when the Führer himself made his entry. Paradoxically, the man who was most affected by such spectacles was their originator, Hitler himself, and, as Rosenberg remarks in his memoirs, they played an indispensable part in the process of self-intoxication.

Hitler had grasped as no one before him what could be done with a combination of propaganda and terrorism. For the complement to the attractive power of the great spectacles was the compulsive power of the Gestapo, the S.S., and the concentration camp, heightened once again by skilful propaganda. Hitler was helped in this not only by his own perception of the sources of power in a modern urbanized mass-society, but also by possession of the technical means to manipulate them. This was a point well made by Albert Speer, Hitler's highly intelligent Minister for Armaments and War Production, in the final speech he made at his trial after the war.

Hitler's dictatorship [Speer told the court] differed in one fundamental point from all its predecessors in history. His was the first dictatorship in the present period of modern technical development, a dictatorship which made complete use of all technical means for the domination of its own country.

Through technical devices like the radio and the loud-speaker, eighty million people were deprived of independent thought. It was thereby possible to subject them to the will of one man. . . .

Earlier dictators needed highly qualified assistants, even at the lowest level, men who would think and act independently. The totalitarian system in the period of modern technical development can dispense with them; the means of communication alone make it possible to mechanize the lower leadership. As a result of this there arises the new type of the uncritical recipient of orders. . . . Another result was the far-reaching supervision of the citizens of the State and the maintenance of a high degree of secrecy for criminal acts.

The nightmare of many a man that one day nations could be dominated by technical means was all but realized in Hitler's totalitarian system.

In making use of the formidable power which was thus placed in his hands Hitler had one supreme, and fortunately rare, advantage: he had neither scruples nor inhibitions. He was a man without roots, with neither home nor family; a man who admitted no loyalties, was bound by no traditions, and felt respect neither for God nor man. Throughout his career Hitler showed himself prepared to seize any advantage that was to be gained by lying, cunning, treachery, and unscrupulousness. He demanded the sacrifice of millions of German lives for the sacred cause of Germany, but in the last year of the war was ready to destroy Germany rather than surrender his power or admit defeat. . . .

He had a particular and inveterate distrust of experts. He refused to be impressed by the complexity of problems, insisting until it became monotonous that if only the will was there any problem could be solved. Schacht, to whose advice he refused to listen and whose admiration was reluctant, says of him: 'Hitler often did find astonishingly simple solutions for problems which had seemed to others insoluble. He had a genius for invention. . . . His solutions were often brutal, but almost always effective.' In an interview with a French correspondent early in 1936 Hitler himself claimed this power of simplification as his greatest gift:

It has been said that I owe my success to the fact that I have created a *mystique* . . . or more simply that I have been lucky. Well, I will tell you what has carried me to the position I have reached. Our political problems appeared complicated. The German people could make nothing of them. In these circumstances they preferred to leave it to the professional politicians to get them out of this confused mess. I, on the other hand, simplified the problems and reduced them to the simplest terms. The masses realized this and followed me.

The crudest of Hitler's simplifications was the most effective: in almost any situation, he believed, force or the threat of force would settle matters—and in an astonishingly large number of cases he proved right.

In his Munich days Hitler always carried a heavy riding-whip, made of hippopotamus hide. The impression he wanted to convey—and every phrase and gesture in his speeches reflected the same purpose—was one of force, decision, will. Yet Hitler had nothing of the easy, assured toughness of a condottiere like Göring. His strength of personality, far from being natural to him, was the product of an exertion of will: from this sprang a harsh, jerky and over-emphatic manner which was very noticeable in his early days as a politician. No word was more frequently on Hitler's lips than 'will,' and his whole career from 1919 to 1945 is a remarkable achievement of will-power.

To say that Hitler was ambitious scarcely describes the intensity of the lust for power and the craving to dominate which consumed him. It was the will to power in its crudest and purest form, not identifying itself with the triumph of a principle as with Lenin or Robespierre—for the only principle of Nazism was power and domination for its own sake—nor finding satisfaction in the fruits of power, for, by comparison with other Nazi leaders like Göring, Hitler lived an ascetic life. For a long time Hitler succeeded in identifying his own power with the recovery of Germany's old position in the world, and there were many in the 1930s who spoke of him as a fanatical patriot. But as soon as the interests of Germany began to diverge from his own, from the beginning of 1943 onwards, his patriotism was seen at its true value—Germany, like everything else in the world, was only a means, a vehicle for his own power, which he would sacrifice with the same indifference as the lives of those he sent to the

Eastern Front. By its nature this was an insatiable appetite, securing only a temporary gratification by the exercise of power, then restlessly demanding an ever further extension of it. . . .

Cynical though he was, Hitler's cynicism stopped short of his own person: he came to believe that he was a man with a mission, marked out by Providence, and therefore exempt from the ordinary canons of human conduct.

Hitler probably held some such belief about himself from an early period. It was clear enough in the speech he made at his trial in 1924, and after he came out of prison those near him noticed that he began to hold aloof, to set a barrier between himself and his followers. After he came to power it became more noticeable. It was in March 1936, that he made the famous assertion: . . . 'I go the way that Providence dictates with the assurance of a sleep-walker.' In 1937 he told an audience at Würzburg:

However weak the individual may be when compared with the omnipotence and will of Providence, yet at the moment when he acts as Providence would have him act he becomes immeasurably strong. Then there streams down upon him that force which has marked all greatness in the world's history. And when I look back only on the five years which lie behind us, then I feel that I am justified in saying: That has not been the work of man alone.

Just before the occupation of Austria, in February 1938, he declared in the Reichstag:

Above all, a man who feels it his duty at such an hour to assume the leadership of his people is not responsible to the laws of parliamentary usage or to a particular democratic conception, but solely to the mission placed upon him. And anyone who interferes with this mission is an enemy of the people.

It was in this sense of mission that Hitler, a man who believed neither in God nor in conscience ('a Jewish invention, a blemish like circumcision'), found both justification and absolution. He was the Siegfried come to reawaken Germany to greatness, for whom morality, suffering and 'the litany of private virtues' were irrelevant. It was by such dreams that he sustained the ruthlessness and determination of his will. So long as this sense of mission was balanced by the cynical calculations of the politician, it represented a source of strength, but success was fatal. When half Europe lay at his feet and all need of restraint was removed, Hitler abandoned himself entirely to megalomania. He became convinced of his own infallibility. But when he began to look to the image he had created to work miracles of its own accord—instead of exploiting it—his gifts deteriorated and his intuition deluded him. Ironically, failure sprang from the same capacity which brought him success, his power of self-dramatization, his ability to convince himself. His belief in his power to work miracles kept him going when the more sceptical Mussolini faltered. Hitler played out his 'world-historical' role to the bitter end. But it was this same belief which curtained him in illusion and blinded him to what was actually happening, leading him into that arrogant overestimate of his own genius which brought him to defeat. The sin which Hitler committed was that which the ancient Greeks called *hybris*, the sin of overweening pride, of believing himself to be more than a man. No man was ever more surely destroyed by the image he had created than Adolf Hitler.

In the preceding selection Bullock gives many
insights into the political talents of Hitler, but he
eschews discussion of the Führer's psychological
make-up. The next two selections provide
such discussion. The first was written by
DOUGLAS M. KELLEY (1912-1958), an American
who served as prison psychiatrist during the Nazi
war trials at Nuremberg. Kelley, of course,
never interviewed Hitler—the only psychiatrist,
a German, who sought to treat him disappeared on
orders of the patient. As prison psychiatrist,
however, Kelley had long conversations with men
who knew Hitler intimately. His diagnosis is
made on the basis of these interviews—notably with
the following Nazi leaders mentioned in the
selection: Dr. Karl Brandt, one of Hitler's personal
physicians; Field Marshall Hermann Göring,
second in command to Hitler and leader of the
German air force; Admiral Karl Doenitz, commander
in chief of the navy; Baldur von Shirach, leader
of the Hitler Youth movement; and Joachim von
Ribbentrop, Nazi foreign minister.*

Hitler: A Compulsive Fanatic

Physically, Hitler weighed about 150
pounds and was five feet nine inches in
height. His skin was pale, and his phy-
sique generally unprepossessing. Medical examinations were essentially normal, and the usual medical procedures
were generally negative. Toward the
end of 1943, he developed some weakness
of the left leg and of the left arm, in
which he also developed increasing trem-
ulousness. He was studied by a number
of physicians, and the symptoms were
diagnosed as hysterical reaction without
actual nerve damage. . . .

Aside from this hysterical reaction,
Hitler presented no physical abnormali-
ties of any type. Hitler's personality,
however, is a much more difficult problem. As one of his physicians unemphat-
ically put it: "His psychic state was very
complex." . . .

In his own private circle, Hitler's behavior was generally genial. No one
crossed him, and he was liked by his
intimates for the usual reasons—kindli-
ness and cordiality. He was especially
friendly toward children and older
people. He had a great understanding
for the little pleasures and in his deal-
ings with women displayed a positive
charm.

Everyone who discussed this point with

* Reprinted with permission from *22 Cells in Nuremberg* by Douglas M. Kelley, copyright 1947
by the author. Chilton Books, Philadelphia and New York. Pp. 204–205, 211–217, 221, 235–236.

me mentioned that Hitler behaved like "a Viennese gentleman"—a German character similar to our "Southern gentleman." This behavior not only included the usual social amenities but an exaggeration of grace. For instance, Hitler made it a point to kiss the hand of any woman to whom he was introduced. He apparently liked to be with women and often demanded, with a minimum of tact, that the most beautiful and interesting sit beside him. Brandt observed that Hitler sometimes became almost coquettish with the feminine sex.

Hitler's ideal of woman was a creature of beauty and intelligence—for the amusement of men at parties and dances. He felt, however, that women's intelligence should not be along political lines; and he often said that, so far as he personally was concerned, he was not interested in women who had original ideas because he himself had "enough ideas for both."

Curiously, according to Brandt who knew her well, Eva Braun—Hitler's favorite and eventually his wife—though pretty, intelligent, and extremely energetic, was somewhat masculine in nature. She dressed most often in sport clothes, and her interests were swimming, skiing, and mountain climbing. Brandt described her character as being harsh rather than womanlike or soft.

Hitler's failure to marry his acknowledged mistress until the last hours of his life has provoked much comment. The explanation, it seems, was political, and it displays an anxiety on Hitler's part lest he lose even sexually incited public support. Both Göring and Schirach, who had parts in the decision against marriage, agreed that it was based on the feeling that an unmarried Hitler had a greater appeal for German women folk than a married Führer would have. Hitler, they said, agreed; and the idea was apparently strongly shared by Goebbels, who made the most of Hitler's bachelorhood in his promotion of "beautiful Adolf."

I am convinced that Hitler was not, overtly, a sexual pervert—as so many biographers have hinted or charged outright. All the evidence I was able to obtain from his physicians and friends indicate that he did manifest less sexual energy than the average man, and was perhaps even what is called a "latent homosexual type"—one with a deeply repressed homosexuality. He made a virtue of this buried sex drive, converting it into the energy that made it possible for him to work eighteen to twenty hours a day.

When I put the question of Hitler's sexual abnormality to Göring, I got, interestingly enough, the flattest of all denials. Göring snorted: "Hitler was just as normal in every way as any normal man."

Along with his superiority feelings, his megalomania, Hitler exhibited some very definite neurotic reactions. One already mentioned was his inability to accept the opinions of others. According to Dr. Brandt, in time "this be-right attitude was followed by an absolute wanting-to-be-right attitude." He came to hate people who knew more than he did, to tolerate those who knew as much and, often, to adore those who knew less.

Doubtless his early military and political successes furnished convincing—for him—evidence that he was and could only be right. When a failure occurred or a mistake was made, it was, Adolf Hitler found it easy to believe, never his fault but always the fault of someone else. During his years as Führer, he became more and more possessed with this idea. It is a typical one in individuals who feel inner insecurity. . . .

These feelings of inferiority can undoubtedly be traced back to the inadequacies of Hitler's early life and the frustrations of his years in Vienna. In overcompensation, he developed a refusal to accept counsel or opinions from others. Another compensatory device was to surround himself with intelligent people and then astound them with his superior knowledge. So long as the device worked, Hitler would seem a calm conversationalist. But if a discussion seemed to be getting away from him, he would become more and more outspoken and his voice would rise until he was outshouting all other voices. . . .

In addition to his feelings of inadequacy, Hitler exhibited other signs of definite neurotic reactions. He suffered from a large number of phobias and compulsions. He had a marked fear of death and, because of it, had up to five physicians in constant attendance. He consistently refused to allow anyone to give him a comprehensive examination. He would never permit X-rays because he feared they might reveal an incurable cancer.

Hitler would seldom touch an animal unless he was wearing gloves. On those occasions when he caressed his dog without gloves, he would immediately go and wash his hands many times. He was apparently fascinated by, but fearful of, horses. He surrounded himself with pictures and tapestries of the finest stallions but refused adamantly to do any actual riding. This is a fairly common reaction in men like Hitler. To him the stallion probably represented a strongly sexually potent animal—all the pictures displayed their sex organs. Hitler surrounded himself with such pictures, enviously admiring their strength and yet actually afraid of the animals themselves, who possessed these qualities which he lacked but most desired. From the pictures, he derived vicarious "sexual strength"—a satisfactory substitute—until faced with the real thing, when the satisfaction turned to hate and fear.

His personal life, while extremely simple, indicates strong persistence of habits. He was extremely clean, bathed frequently, and offered as his reason for being a vegetarian that eating meat caused his perspiration—which poured off him during his speeches—to smell bad. He did not drink and gave up smoking during his student days in Vienna. In fact, he came to dislike tobacco so much that no smoking was permitted in his presence, and he often commented on the disagreeable odor of those who had a taint of tobacco smoke on their clothes.

His daily routines were strict and were followed to the minutest degree. All his intimates agreed on this. Whenever he took a walk, it was—if feasible—always the very same walk he had taken the day before. If he took his dog across a field and threw a piece of wood for the dog to retrieve, the next day he would throw the piece from exactly the same spot and in the same direction. Each day the dog had to sit down at the same place and wait until Hitler sent him to get the stick. That exact procedure would be repeated day after day until the animal finally would go through the routine without a word from his master. . . .

He was more than meticulous about his clothing, particularly his linen. If at any time he got a spot on his collar, he would at once bathe and change all his clothing, including his underwear. He avoided everything he could of a soiling nature, cleaning his teeth immediately after eating anything and washing his hands many times each day.

Such behavior, generated through a fear of dirt or disease germs, is typical of many obsessive compulsive neuroses. In Hitler this obsessive pattern was part of his basic structure, having been established early in childhood. It can be considered as not severe, since his compulsions did not actually interfere to any great degree with his daily life.

On the other hand, such actions are most revealing in emphasizing the basic structure of his nature. It is this obsession-compulsion component that drove him on to his final destruction. Because of the rigidity of his personality, typical in such characters, he was unable to shift his goals—even when they obviously led only to failure and death.

His obsessive beliefs forced him into quick decisions. For example, his fear of stomach cancer, a purely neurotic obsession, caused him to turn from a fairly successful campaign against Britain to the hopeless Russian debacle. Göring's explanation was that Hitler felt he might soon die (obsessive fear) and consequently, since he was the only one who could successfully fight against communism (compulsive drive), Russia must be attacked immediately. The horrors of this decision are well known, and it is appalling to realize that an entire war was precipitated because of the severe hysterical stomach cramps and obsessive-compulsive fears of a psychoneurotic who happened to be in a position of command. . . .

In discussing him with many individuals, I concluded that he had many faces and that many of his followers were apparently unaware of any but the facade which he had presented to them. He seemed to permit each individual to project upon him that type of personality which that individual most respected and admired. With Göring he was friendly, outspoken and blunt; with Doenitz he was simple, intellectual and quiet; with Schirach he was a dominat-

ing authority; and with Ribbentrop he was a father and a master. . . .

In summary, from a medical viewpoint, we would diagnose Adolf Hitler as an individual who in early life suffered from marked frustration and, as a result, suffered definite feelings of inferiority throughout the remainder of his career. In order to overcome these feelings, he developed an over-compensation, which finally culminated in actual belief in his own superiority and Divine mission on earth. He would be classified as a psychoneurotic of the obsessive and hysterical type, and these obsessive and compulsive patterns, driving along lines of hyper-compensation, forced him into situations from which he could not withdraw; and the development of these situations resulted in the war. In addition, he had definite hysterical symptoms as manifested by his stomach complaints, his outbursts of anger, and his hysterical paralysis of his left side. Basically, he also showed paranoid or persecution patterns, manifested by his marked suspiciousness and his feelings, both for himself and for Germany, that every nation and people was persecuting him. Other evidence of his paranoid and persecution patterns was his projection on to others of the blame for anything untoward that happened in the Third Reich.

In simple terms, Hitler was an abnormal and a mentally ill individual, though his deviations were not of a nature which in the average individual would arouse the serious concern of others. He was able, by his drive, his intelligence, and his ability in handling people, to reach a position where, in the end, his pathological deviations could disrupt and almost destroy the entire civilized world.

ERICH FROMM (1900–   ), a leading American psychoanalyst, has written widely on problems of personal and social abnormality. In this selection he adds a new dimension to the study of Hitler and of Nazi Germany. He argues that Hitler's very pathology was directly related to his success in attracting the support of the German people. Fromm's interpretation serves as a bridge to the next section in this book of readings, which deals with the question of why Hitler came to power.*

Hitler's Personality: The Basis of His Appeal

In the following pages we shall try to show that Hitler's personality, his teachings, and the Nazi system express an extreme form of the character structure which we have called "authoritarian" and that by this very fact he made a powerful appeal to those parts of the population which were—more or less—of the same character structure.

Hitler's autobiography is as good an illustration of the authoritarian character as any, and since in addition to that it is the most representative document of Nazi literature I shall use it as the main source for analyzing the psychology of Nazism.

The essence of the authoritarian character is the simultaneous presence of sadistic and masochistic drives. Sadism is understood as aiming at unrestricted power over another person more or less mixed with destructiveness; masochism as aiming at dissolving oneself in an overwhelmingly strong power and participating in its strength and glory. Both the sadistic and the masochistic trends are caused by the inability of the isolated individual to stand alone and his need for a symbiotic relationship that overcomes this aloneness.

The *sadistic craving for power* finds manifold expressions in *Mein Kampf*. It is characteristic of Hitler's relationship to the German masses whom he despises and "loves" in the typically sadistic manner, as well as to his political enemies towards whom he evidences those destructive elements that are an

* From *Escape from Freedom* by Erich Fromm. Copyright 1941 by Erich Fromm. Reprinted by permission of Holt, Rinehart and Winston, Inc., and Routledge & Kegan Paul Ltd. Pp. 221–223, 225–237.

important component of his sadism. He speaks of the satisfaction the masses have in domination. "What they want is the victory of the stronger and the annihilation or the unconditional surrender of the weaker." "Like a woman, . . . who will submit to the strong man rather than dominate the weakling, thus the masses love the ruler rather than the suppliant, and inwardly they are far more satisfied by a doctrine which tolerates no rival than by the grant of liberal freedom; they often feel at a loss what to do with it, and even easily feel themselves deserted. They neither realize the impudence with which they are spiritually terrorized, nor the outrageous curtailment of their human liberties for in no way does the delusion of this doctrine dawn on them."

He describes the breaking of the will of the audience by the superior strength of the speaker as the essential factor in propaganda. He does not even hesitate to admit that physical tiredness of his audience is a most welcome condition for their suggestibility. Discussing the question which hour of the day is most suited for political mass meetings he says: "It seems that in the morning and even during the day men's will power revolts with highest energy against an attempt at being forced under another's will and another's opinion. In the evening, however, they succumb more easily to the dominating force of a stronger will. For truly every such meeting presents a wrestling match between two opposed forces. The superior oratorical talent of a domineering apostolic nature will now succeed more easily in winning for the new will people who themselves have in turn experienced a weakening of their force of resistance in the most natural way, than people who still have full command of the energies of their minds and their will power."

Hitler himself is very much aware of the conditions which make for the longing for submission and gives an excellent description of the situation of the individual attending a mass meeting.

"The mass meeting is necessary if only for the reason that in it the individual, who in becoming an adherent of a new movement feels lonely and is easily seized with the fear of being alone, receives for the first time the pictures of a greater community, something that has a strengthening and encouraging effect on most people. . . . If he steps for the first time out of his small workshop or out of the big enterprise, in which he feels very small, into the mass meeting and is now surrounded by thousands and thousands of people with the same conviction . . . he himself succumbs to the magic influence of what we call mass suggestion". . . .

While the "leaders" are the ones to enjoy power in the first place, the masses are by no means deprived of sadistic satisfaction. Racial and political minorities within Germany and eventually other nations which are described as weak or decaying are the objects of sadism upon which the masses are fed. While Hitler and his bureaucracy enjoy the power over the German masses, these masses themselves are taught to enjoy power over other nations and to be driven by the passion for domination of the world.

Hitler does not hesitate to express the wish for world domination as his or his party's aim. Making fun of pacifism, he says: "Indeed, the pacifist-humane idea is perhaps quite good whenever the man of the highest standard has previously conquered and subjected the world to a degree that makes him the only master of this globe."

Again he says: "A state which in the epoch of race poisoning dedicates itself to the cherishing of its best racial elements, must some day be master of the world." . . .

The . . . rationalization, that his wish for power is rooted in the laws of nature, is more than a mere rationalization; it also springs from the wish for submission to a power outside of oneself, as expressed particularly in Hitler's crude popularization of Darwinism. In "the instinct of preserving the species," Hitler sees "the first cause of the formation of human communities." . . . He projects his own sadism upon Nature who is "the cruel Queen of all Wisdom," and her law of preservation is "bound to the brazen law of necessity and of the right of the victory of the best and the strongest in this world."

It is interesting to observe that in connection with this crude Darwinism the "socialist" Hitler champions the liberal principles of unrestricted competition. In a polemic against co-operation between different nationalistic groups he says: "By such a combination the free play of energies is tied up, the struggle for choosing the best is stopped, and accordingly the necessary and final victory of the healthier and stronger man is prevented forever." Elsewhere he speaks of the free play of energies as the wisdom of life. . . .

The last rationalization for his sadism, his justification of it as a defense against attacks of others, finds manifold expressions in Hitler's writings. He and the German people are always the ones who are innocent and the enemies are sadistic brutes. A great deal of this propaganda consists of deliberate, conscious lies. Partly, however, it has the same emotional "sincerity" which paranoid accusations have. These accusations always have the function of a defense against being found out with regard to one's own sadism or destructiveness. They

run according to the formula: It is you who have sadistic intention. Therefore I am innocent. With Hitler this defensive mechanism is irrational to the extreme, since he accuses his enemies of the very things he quite frankly admits to be his own aims. Thus he accuses the Jews, the Communists, and the French of the very things that he says are the most legitimate aims of his own actions. He scarcely bothers to cover this contradiction by rationalizations. He accuses the Jews of bringing the French African troops to the Rhine with the intention to destroy, by the bastardization which would necessarily set in, the white race and thus "in turn to rise personally to the position of master." Hitler must have detected the contradiction of condemning others for that which he claims to be the most noble aim of his race, and he tries to rationalize the contradiction by saying of the Jews that *their* instinct for self-preservation lacks the idealistic character which is to be found in the Aryan drive for mastery. . . .

The Communists are accused of brutality and the success of Marxism is attributed to its political will and activistic brutality. At the same time, however, Hiler declares: "What Germany was lacking was a close co-operation of brutal power and ingenious political intention."

. . . The love for the powerful and the hatred for the powerless which is so typical for the sado-masochistic character explains a great deal of Hitler's and his followers' political actions. While the Republican government thought they could "appease" the Nazis by treating them leniently, they not only failed to appease them but aroused their hatred by the very lack of power and firmness they showed. Hitler hated the Weimar Republic *because* it was weak and he admired the industrial and military leaders because they had power. . . . As long as he felt Britain to be powerful, he loved and admired her. His book gives expression to this love for Britain. When he recognized the weakness of the British position before and after Munich his love changed into hatred and the wish to destroy it. From this viewpoint "appeasement" was a policy which for a personality like Hitler was bound to arouse hatred, not friendship.

So far we have spoken of the *sadistic* side in Hitler's ideology. However, as we have seen in the discussion of the authoritarian character, there is the *masochistic* side as well as the sadistic one. There is the wish to submit to an overwhelmingly strong power, to annihilate the self, besides the wish to have power over helpless beings. This masochistic side of the Nazi ideology and practice is most obvious with respect to the masses. They are told again and again: the individual is nothing and does not count. The individual should accept his personal insignificance, dissolve himself in a higher power, and then feel proud in participating in the strength and glory of this higher power. Hitler expresses this idea clearly in his definition of idealism: "Idealism alone leads men to voluntary acknowledgment of the privilege of force and strength and thus makes them become a dust particle of that order which forms and shapes the entire universe". . . .

It is the aim of education to teach the individual not to assert his self. Already the boy in school must learn "to be silent, not only when he is blamed justly but he has also to learn, if necessary, to bear injustice in silence." . . .

This whole preaching of self-sacrifice has an obvious purpose: The masses have to resign themselves and submit if the wish for power on the side of the leader and the "elite" is to be realized.

But this masochistic longing is also to be found in Hitler himself. For him the superior power to which he submits is God, Fate, Necessity, History, Nature. Actually all these terms have about the same meaning to him, that of symbols of an overwhelmingly strong power. . . .

I have tried to show in Hitler's writings the two trends that we have already described as fundamental for the authoritarian character: the craving for power over men and the longing for submission to an overwhelmingly strong outside power. Hitler's ideas are more or less identical with the ideology of the Nazi party. The ideas expressed in his book are those which he expressed in the countless speeches by which he won mass following for his party. This ideology results from his personality which, with its inferiority feeling, hatred against life, asceticism, and envy of those who enjoy life, is the soil of sado-masochistic strivings; it was addressed to people who, on account of their similar character structure, felt attracted and excited by these teachings and became ardent followers of the man who expressed what they felt. But it was not only the Nazi ideology that satisfied the lower middle class; the political practice realized what the ideology promised. A hierarchy was created in which everyone has somebody above him to submit to and somebody beneath him to feel power over; the man at the top, the leader, has Fate, History, Nature above him as the power in which to submerge himself. Thus the Nazi ideology and practice satisfies the desires springing from the character structure of one part of the population and gives direction and orientation to those who, though not enjoying domination and submission, were resigned and had given up faith in life, in their own decisions, in everything.

This selection presents a widely held view about
the causes of Nazism: its roots lay deep in
German history. WILLIAM L. SHIRER (1904–   )
is one of America's best known foreign correspondents
and news commentators. Millions of people
listened avidly to his radio broadcasts from Berlin
during the Hitler period, and his history of the
Third Reich became a best seller. The central
thesis of the book is given here; it is taken
from the chapter, "The Mind of Hitler and
the Roots of the Third Reich."*

Nazism: A Continuation of German History

The mind and the passion of Hitler—
all the aberrations that possessed his
feverish brain—had roots that lay deep
in German experience and thought.
Nazism and the Third Reich, in fact,
were but a logical continuation of German history. . . .

There is not space in this book to re-
count adequately the immense influence
that Martin Luther, the Saxon peasant
who became an Augustinian monk and
launched the German Reformation, had
on the Germans and their subsequent
history. But it may be said, in passing,
that this towering but erratic genius,
this savage anti-Semite and hater of
Rome, who combined in his tempestuous
character so many of the best and the
worst qualities of the German—the

coarseness, the boisterousness, the fanaticism, the intolerance, the violence, but
also the honesty, the simplicity, the self-
scrutiny, the passion for learning and
for music and for poetry and for righ-
teousness in the eyes of God—left a mark
on the life of the Germans, for both good
and bad, more indelible, more fateful,
than was wrought by any other single
individual before or since. Through his
sermons and his magnificent translation
of the Bible, Luther created the modern
German language, aroused in the people
not only a new Protestant vision of
Christianity but a fervent German nationalism and taught them, at least in
religion, the supremacy of the individual
conscience. But tragically for them,
Luther's siding with the princes in the

* From William L. Shirer, *The Rise and Fall of the Third Reich: A History of Nazi Germany*
(New York, 1960), pp. 90–102, 111, 113. Copyright © 1959, 1960, by William L. Shirer. Reprinted by
permission of Simon and Schuster, Inc., and Martin Secker & Warburg Limited.

29

peasant risings, which he had largely inspired, and his passion for political autocracy ensured a mindless and provincial political absolutism which reduced
the vast majority of the German people
to poverty, to a horrible torpor and a
demeaning subservience. Even worse
perhaps, it helped to perpetuate and indeed to sharpen the hopeless divisions
not only between classes but also between the various dynastic and political
groupings of the German people. It
doomed for centuries the possibility of
the unification of Germany.

The Thirty Years' War and Peace of
Westphalia of 1648, which ended it,
brought the final catastrophe to Germany, a blow so devastating that the
country has never fully recovered from
it. . . .

Acceptance of autocracy, of blind obedience to the petty tyrants who ruled as
princes, became ingrained in the German
mind. The idea of democracy, of rule
by parliament, which made such rapid
headway in England in the seventeenth
and eighteenth centuries, and which exploded in France in 1789, did not sprout
in Germany. This political backwardness of the Germans, divided as they
were into so many petty states and isolated in them from the surging currents
of European thought and development,
set Germany apart from and behind the
other countries of the West. There was
no natural growth of a nation. This has
to be borne in mind if one is to comprehend the disastrous road this people subsequently took and the warped state of
mind which settled over it. In the end
the German nation was forged by naked
force and held together by naked aggression.

Beyond the Elbe to the east lay Prussia. As the nineteenth century waned,
this century which had seen the sorry

failure of the confused and timid liberals
at Frankfurt in 1848–49 to create a somewhat democratic, unified Germany, Prussia took over the German destiny. For
centuries this Germanic state had lain
outside the main stream of German historical development and culture. It
seemed almost as if it were a freak of
history. Prussia had begun as the remote
frontier state of Brandenburg on the
sandy wastes east of the Elbe which, beginning with the eleventh century, had
been slowly conquered from the Slavs.
Under Brandenburg's ruling princes, the
Hohenzollerns, who were little more
than military adventurers, the Slavs,
mostly Poles, were gradually pushed back
along the Baltic. Those who resisted
were either exterminated or made landless serfs. . . . By a supreme act of will
and a genius for organization the Hohenzollerns managed to create a Spartan
military state whose well-drilled Army
won one victory after another and whose
Machiavellian diplomacy of temporary
alliances with whatever power seemed
the strongest brought constant additions
to its territory.

There thus arose quite artificially a
state born of no popular force nor even
of an idea except that of conquest, and
held together by the absolute power of
the ruler, by a narrow-minded bureaucracy which did his bidding and by
a ruthlessly disciplined army. Two
thirds and sometimes as much as five
sixths of the annual state revenue was
expended on the Army, which became,
under the King, the state itself. "Prussia," remarked Mirabeau, "is not a state
with any army, but an army with a
state." And the state, which was run
with the efficiency and soullessness of a
factory, became all; the people were
little more than cogs in the machinery.
Individuals were taught not only by the
kings and the drill sergeants but by the

philosophers that their role in life was one of obedience, work, sacrifice and duty. Even Kant preached that duty demands the suppression of human feeling, and the Prussian poet Willibald Alexis gloried in the enslavement of the people under the Hohenzollerns. To Lessing, who did not like it, "Prussia was the most slavish country of Europe."

The Junkers, who were to play such a vital role in modern Germany, were also a unique product of Prussia. They were, as they said, a master race. It was they who occupied the land conquered from the Slavs and who farmed it on large estates worked by these Slavs, who became landless serfs quite different from those in the West. There was an essential difference between the agrarian system in Prussia and that of western Germany and Western Europe. In the latter, the nobles, who owned most of the land, received rents or feudal dues from the peasants, who though often kept in a state of serfdom had certain rights and privileges and could, and did, gradually acquire their own land and civic freedom. In the West, the peasants formed a solid part of the community; the landlords, for all their drawbacks, developed in their leisure a cultivation which led to, among other things, a civilized quality of life that could be seen in the refinement of manners, of thought and of the arts.

The Prussian Junker was not a man of leisure. He worked hard at managing his large estate, much as a factory manager does today. His landless laborers were treated as virtual slaves. On his large properties he was the absolute lord. There were no large towns nor any substantial middle class, as there were in the West, whose civilizing influence might rub against him. In contrast to the cultivated *grand seigneur* in the West, the Junker developed into a rude, domineering, arrogant type of man, without cultivation or culture, aggressive, conceited, ruthless, narrow-minded and given to a petty profit-seeking that some German historians noted in the private life of Otto von Bismarck, the most successful of the Junkers.

It was this political genius, this apostle of "blood and iron," who between 1866 and 1871 brought an end to a divided Germany which had existed for nearly a thousand years and, by force, replaced it with Greater Prussia, or what might be called Prussian Germany. Bismarck's unique creation is the Germany we have known in our time, a problem child of Europe and the world for nearly a century, a nation of gifted, vigorous people in which first this remarkable man and then Kaiser Wilhelm II and finally Hitler, aided by a military caste and by many a strange intellectual, succeeded in inculcating a lust for power and domination, a passion for unbridled militarism, a contempt for democracy and individual freedom and a longing for authority, for authoritarianism. . . .

"The great questions of the day," Bismarck declared on becoming Prime Minister of Prussia in 1862, "will not be settled by resolutions and majority votes —that was the mistake of the men of 1848 and 1849—but by blood and iron." That was exactly the way he proceeded to settle them, though it must be said that he added a touch of diplomatic finesse, often of the most deceitful kind. Bismarck's aim was to destroy liberalism, bolster the power of conservatism—that is, of the Junkers, the Army and the crown—and make Prussia, as against Austria, the dominant power not only among the Germans but, if possible, in Europe as well. "Germany looks not to Prussia's liberalism," he told the deputies in the Prussian parliament, "but to her force." . . .

Bismarck's crowning achievement, the creation of the Second Reich, came on January 18, 1871, when King Wilhelm I of Prussia was proclaimed Emperor of Germany in the Hall of Mirrors at Versailles. Germany had been unified by Prussian armed force. It was now the greatest power on the Continent; its only rival in Europe was England.

Yet there was a fatal flaw. The German Empire, as Treitschke said, was in reality but an extension of Prussia. "Prussia," he emphasized, "is the dominant factor . . . The will of the Empire can be nothing but the will of the Prussian state." This was true, and it was to have disastrous consequences for the Germans themselves. From 1871 to 1933 and indeed to Hitler's end in 1945, the course of German history as a consequence was to run, with the exception of the interim of the Weimar Republic, in a straight line and with utter logic.

Despite the democratic facade put up by the establishment of the Reichstag, whose members were elected by universal manhood suffrage, the German Empire was in reality a militarist autocracy ruled by the King of Prussia, who was also Emperor. The Reichstag possessed few powers; it was little more than a debating society where the representatives of the people let off steam or bargained for shoddy benefits for the classes they represented. The throne had the power—by divine right. As late as 1910 Wilhelm II could proclaim that the royal crown had been "granted by God's Grace alone and not by parliaments, popular assemblies and popular decision . . . Considering myself an instrument of the Lord," he added, "I go my way."

He was not impeded by Parliament. The Chancellor he appointed was responsible to him, not to the Reichstag. The assembly could not overthrow a Chancellor nor keep him in office. That was the prerogative of the monarch. Thus, in contrast to the development in other countries in the West, the idea of democracy, of the people sovereign, of the supremacy of parliament, never got a foothold in Germany, even after the twentieth century began. To be sure, the Social Democrats, after years of persecution by Bismarck and the Emperor, had become the largest single political party in the Reichstag by 1912. They loudly demanded the establishment of a parliamentary democracy. But they were ineffective. And, though the largest party, they were still a minority. The middle classes, grown prosperous by the belated but staggering development of the industrial revolution and dazzled by the success of Bismarck's policy of force and war, had traded for material gain any aspirations for political freedom they may have had.[1] They accepted the Hohenzollern autocracy. They gladly knuckled under to the Junker bureaucracy and they fervently embraced Prussian militarism. Germany's star had risen and they—almost all the people— were eager to do what their masters asked to keep it high.

At the very end, Hitler, the Austrian,

[1] In a sense the German working class made a similar trade. To combat socialism Bismarck put through between 1883 and 1889 a program for social security far beyond anything known in other countries. It included compulsory insurance for workers against old age, sickness, accident and incapacity, and though organized by the State it was financed by employers and employees. It cannot be said that it stopped the rise of the Social Democrats or the trade unions, but it did have a profound influence on the working class in that it gradually made them value security over political freedom and caused them to see in the State, however conservative, a benefactor and a protector. Hitler, as we shall see, took full advantage of this state of mind. In this, as in other matters, he learned much from Bismarck. "I studied Bismarck's socialist legislation," Hitler remarks in *Mein Kampf* (p. 155), "in its intention, struggle and success."

was one of them. To him Bismarck's Second Reich, despite its mistakes and its "terrifying forces of decay" was a work of splendor in which the Germans at last had come into their own. . . .

That was the Germany which Hitler resolved to restore. In *Mein Kampf* he discourses at great length on what he believes are the reasons for its fall: its tolerance of Jews and Marxists, the crass materialism and selfishness of the middle class, the nefarious influence of the "cringers and lickspittles" around the Hohenzollern throne, the "catastrophic German alliance policy" which linked Germany to the degenerate Hapsburgs and the untrustworthy Italians instead of with England, and the lack of a fundamental "social" and racial policy. These were failures which, he promised, National Socialism would correct.

But aside from history, where did Hitler get his ideas? Though his opponents inside and outside Germany were too busy, or too stupid, to take much notice of it until it was too late, he had somehow absorbed, as had so many Germans, a weird mixture of the irresponsible, megalomaniacal ideas which erupted from German thinkers during the nineteenth century. Hitler, who often got them at second hand through such a muddled pseudo philosopher as Alfred Rosenberg or through his drunken poet friend Dietrich Eckart, embraced them with all the feverish enthusiasm of a neophyte. What was worse, he resolved to put them into practice if the opportunity should ever arise.

We have seen what they were as they thrashed about in Hitler's mind: the glorification of war and conquest and the absolute power of the authoritarian state; the belief in the Aryans, or Germans, as the master race, and the hatred of Jews and Slavs; the contempt for democracy and humanism. They are not

original with Hitler—though the means of applying them later proved to be. They emanate from the odd assortment of erudite but unbalanced philosophers, historians and teachers who captured the German mind during the century before Hitler with consequences so disastrous, as it turned out, not only for the Germans but for a large portion of mankind.

There had been among the Germans, to be sure, some of the most elevated minds and spirits of the Western world—Leibnitz, Kant, Herder, Humboldt, Lessing, Goethe, Schiller, Bach, and Beethoven—and they had made unique contributions to the civilization of the West. But the German culture which became dominant in the nineteenth century and which coincided with the rise of Prussian Germany, continuing from Bismarck through Hitler, rests primarily on Fichte and Hegel, to begin with, and then on Treitschke, Nietzsche, Richard Wagner, and a host of lesser lights not the least of whom, strangely enough, were a bizarre Frenchman and an eccentric Englishman.[2] They succeeded in establishing a spiritual break with the West; the breach has not been healed to this day.

In 1807, following Prussia s humiliating defeat by Napoleon at Jena, Johann

[2] Shirer refers to Count Joseph Arthur de Gobineau, a French aristocrat, diplomatist, and writer whose four-volume work insisted that the key to understanding all history and civilization was provided by a study of race. To him, the white race was the master people and among the white race, the Aryans were the elite. His work was entitled *Essai sur l'Inégalité des Races Humaines* (Paris, 1853–1855). The "eccentric Englishman" was Houston Stewart Chamberlain, a highly neurotic admirer of Gobineau, who was given to seeing demons and thought himself a type of messiah. In his racist book, *Die Grundlagen des Neunzehnten Jahrhunderts* [*The Foundations of the Nineteenth Century*] (Vienna, 1899), he sought to prove—among other things—that Jesus was not a Jew. Chamberlain was Richard Wagner's son-in-law.—*Ed.*

Gottlieb Fichte began his famous "Addresses to the German Nation" from the podium of the University of Berlin, where he held the chair of philosophy. They stirred and rallied a divided, defeated people and their resounding echoes could still be heard in the Third Reich. Fichte's teaching was heady wine for a frustrated folk. To him the Latins, especially the French, and the Jews are the decadent races. Only the Germans possess the possibility of regeneration. Their language is the purest, the most original. Under them a new era in history would blossom. It would reflect the order of the cosmos. It would be led by a small elite which would be free of any moral restraints of a "private" nature. These are some of the ideas [Hitler put down] . . . in *Mein Kampf*.

On Fichte's death in 1814, he was succeeded by Georg Wilhelm Friedrich Hegel at the University of Berlin.* This is the subtle and penetrating mind whose dialectics inspired Marx and Lenin and thus contributed to the founding of Communism and whose ringing glorification of the State as supreme in human life paved the way for the Second and Third Reichs of Bismarck and Hitler. To Hegel the State is all, or almost all. Among other things, he says, it is the highest revelation of the "world spirit"; it is the "moral universe"; it is "the actuality of the ethical idea . . . ethical mind . . . knowing and thinking itself"; the State "has the supreme right against the individual, whose supreme duty is to be a member of the State . . . for the right of the world spirit is above all special privileges . . ."

And the happiness of the individual on earth? Hegel replies that "world history is no empire of happiness. The periods of happiness," he declares, "are the empty pages of history because they are the periods of agreement, without

* Actually Hegel did not go to the University of Berlin until 1818.—*Ed.*

conflict." War is the great purifier. In Hegel's view, it makes for "the ethical health of peoples corrupted by a long peace, as the blowing of the winds preserves the sea from the foulness which would be the result of a prolonged calm."

No traditional conception of morals and ethics must disturb either the supreme State or the "heroes" who lead it. "World history occupies a higher ground . . . Moral claims which are irrelevant must not be brought into collision with world-historical deeds and their accomplishments. The litany of private virtues —modesty, humility, philanthropy and forbearance—must not be raised against them . . . So mighty a form [the State] must trample down many an innocent flower—crush to pieces many an object in its path."

Hegel foresees such a State for Germany when she has recovered her God-given genius. He predicts that "Germany's hour" will come and that its mission will be to regenerate the world. As one reads Hegel one realizes how much inspiration Hitler, like Marx, drew from him, even if it was at second hand. Above all else, Hegel in his theory of "heroes," those great agents who are fated by a mysterious Providence to carry out "the will of the world spirit," seems to have inspired Hitler, as we shall see . . . , with his own overpowering sense of mission.

Heinrich von Treitschke came later to the University of Berlin. From 1874 until his death in 1896 he was a professor of history there and a popular one, his lectures being attended by large and enthusiastic gatherings which included not only students but General Staff officers and officials of the Junker bureaucracy. His influence on German thought in the last quarter of the century was enormous and it continued through

Wilhelm II's day and indeed Hitler's. Though he was a Saxon, he became the great Prussianizer; he was more Prussian than the Prussians. Like Hegel he glorifies the State and conceives of it as supreme, but his attitude is more brutish: the people, the subjects, are to be little more than slaves in the nation. "It does not matter what you think," he exclaims, "so long as you obey."

And Treitschke outdoes Hegel in proclaiming war as the highest expression of man. To him "martial glory is the basis of all the political virtues; in the rich treasure of Germany's glories the Prussian military glory is a jewel as precious as the masterpieces of our poets and thinkers." He holds that "to play blindly with peace . . . has become the shame of the thought and morality of our age."

War is not only a practical necessity, it is also a theoretical necessity, an exigency of logic. The concept of the State implies the concept of war, for the essence of the State is power . . . That war should ever be banished from the world is a hope not only absurd, but profoundly immoral. It would involve the atrophy of many of the essential and sublime forces of the human soul . . . A people which become attached to the chimerical hope of perpetual peace finishes irremediably by decaying in its proud isolation . . ."

Nietzsche, like Goethe, held no high opinion of the German people,[3] and in other ways, too, the outpourings of this

[3] "I have often felt," Goethe once said, "a bitter sorrow at the thought of the German people, which is so estimable in the individual and so wretched in the generality. A comparison of the German people with other peoples arouses a painful feeling, which I try to overcome in every possible way." (Conversation with H. Luden on December 13, 1813, in *Goethes Gespraeche,* Auswahl Biedermann; quoted by Wilhelm Roepke in *The Solution of the German Problem,* p. 131.)

megalomaniacal genius differ from those of the chauvinistic German thinkers of the nineteenth century. Indeed, he regarded most German philosophers, including Fichte and Hegel, as "unconscious swindlers." He poked fun at the "Tartuffery of old Kant." The Germans, he wrote in *Ecce Homo,* "have no conception how vile they are," and he came to the conclusion that "whatsoever Germany penetrated, she ruins culture." He thought that Christians, as much as Jews, were responsible for the "slave morality" prevalent in the world; he was never an anti-Semite. He was sometimes fearful of Prussia's future, and in his last years, before insanity closed down his mind, he even toyed with the idea of European union and world government.

Yet I think no one who lived in the Third Reich could have failed to be impressed by Nietzsche's influence on it. His books might be full, as Santayana said, of "genial imbecility" and "boyish blasphemies." Yet Nazi scribblers never tired of extolling him. Hitler often visited the Nietzsche museum in Weimar and publicized his veneration for the philosopher by posing for photographs of himself staring in rapture at the bust of the great man.

There was some ground for this appropriation of Nietzsche as one of the originators of the Nazi *Weltanschauung* [outlook on life]. Had not the philosopher thundered against democracy and parliaments, preached the will to power, praised war and proclaimed the coming of the master race and the superman— and in the most telling aphorisms? A Nazi could proudly quote him on almost every conceivable subject, and did. On Christianity: "the one great curse, the one enormous and innermost perversion . . . I call it the one immortal blemish of mankind . . . This Christianity is no more than the typical teaching of the

Socialists." On the State, power and the jungle world of man: "Society has never regarded virtue as anything else than as a means to strength, power and order. The State [is] unmorality organized . . . the will to war, to conquest and revenge . . . Society is not entitled to exist for its own sake but only as a sub-structure and scaffolding, by means of which a select race of beings may elevate themselves to their higher duties . . . There is no such thing as the right to live, the right to work, or the right to be happy: in this respect man is no different from the meanest worm."[4] And he exalted the superman as the beast of prey, "the magnificent blond brute, avidly rampant for spoil and victory."

And war? Here Nietzsche took the view of most of the other nineteenth-century German thinkers. In the thundering Old Testament language in which *Thus Spake Zarathustra* is written, the philosopher cries out: "Ye shall love peace as a means to new war, and the short peace more than the long. You I advise not to work, but to fight. You I advise not to peace but to victory . . . Ye say it is the good cause which halloweth even war? I say unto you: it is the good war which halloweth every cause. War and courage have done more great things than charity."

Finally there was Nietzsche's prophecy of the coming elite who would rule the

---

[4] Women, whom Nietzsche never had, he consigned to a distinctly inferior status, as did the Nazis, who decreed that their place was in the kitchen and their chief role in life to beget children for German warriors. Nietzsche put the idea this way: "Man shall be trained for war and woman for the procreation of the warrior. All else is folly." He went further. In *Thus Spake Zarathustra* he exclaims: "Thou goest to woman? Do not forget the whip!"—which prompted Bertrand Russell to quip, "Nine women out of ten would have got the whip away from him, and he knew it, so he kept away from women . . ."

world and from whom the superman would spring. In *The Will to Power* he exclaims: "A daring and ruler race is building itself up . . . The aim should be to prepare a transvaluation of values for a particularly strong kind of man, most highly gifted in intellect and will. This man and the elite around him will become the "lords of the earth."

Such rantings from one of Germany's most original minds must have struck a responsive chord in Hitler's littered mind. At any rate he appropriated them for his own—not only the thoughts but the philosopher's penchant for grotesque exaggeration, and often his very words. "Lords of the Earth" is a familiar expression in *Mein Kampf*. That in the end Hitler considered himself the superman of Nietzsche's prophecy can not be doubted.

"Whoever wants to understand National Socialist Germany must know Wagner," Hitler used to say. This may have been based on a partial misconception of the great composer, for though Richard Wagner harbored a fanatical hatred, as Hitler did, for the Jews, who he was convinced were out to dominate the world with their money, and though he scorned parliaments and democracy and the materialism and mediocrity of the bourgeoisie, he also fervently hoped that the Germans, "with their special gifts," would "become not rulers, but ennoblers of the world."

It was not his political writings, however, but his towering operas, recalling so vividly the world of German antiquity with its heroic myths, its fighting pagan gods and heroes, its demons and dragons, its blood feuds and primitive tribal codes, its sense of destiny, of the splendor of love and life and the nobility of death, which inspired the myths of modern Germany and gave it a Germanic

Weltanschauung which Hitler and the Nazis, with some justification, took over as their own.

From his earliest days Hitler worshiped Wagner, and even as his life neared a close, in the damp and dreary bunker at Army headquarters on the Russian front, with his world and his dreams beginning to crack and crumble, he loved to reminisce about all the times he had heard the great Wagnerian works, of what they had meant to him and of the inspiration he had derived from the Bayreuth Festival and from his countless visits to Haus Wahnfried, the composer's home, where Siegfried Wagner, the composer's son, still lived with his English-born wife, Winifred, who for a while was one of his revered friends.

"What joy each of Wagner's works has given me!" Hitler exclaims on the evening of January 24–25, 1942, soon after the first disastrous German defeats in Russia, as he discourses to his generals and party cronies, Himmler among them, in the depths of the underground shelter of Wolfsschanze at Rastenburg in East Prussia. . . .

In Hitler's utterances there runs the theme that the supreme leader is above the morals of ordinary man. Hegel and Nietzsche thought so too. We have seen Hegel's argument that "the private virtues" and "irrelevant moral claims" must not stand in the way of the great rulers, nor must one be squeamish if the heroes, in fulfilling their destiny, trample or "crush to pieces" many an innocent flower. Nietzsche, with his grotesque exaggeration, goes much further.

The strong men, the masters, regain the pure conscience of a beast of prey; monsters filled with joy, they can return from a fearful succession of murder, arson, rape and torture with the same joy in their hearts, the same contentment in their souls as if they had indulged in some student's rag . . . When a man is capable of commanding, when he is by nature a "Master," when he is violent in act and gesture, of what importance are treaties to him? . . . To judge morality properly, it must be replaced by two concepts borrowed from zoology: the *taming* of a beast and the *breeding* of a specific species.

Such teachings, carried to their extremity by Nietzsche and applauded by a host of lesser Germans, seem to have exerted a strong appeal on Hitler. A genius with a mission was above the law; he could not be bound by "bourgeois" morals. Thus, when his time for action came, Hitler could justify the most ruthless and cold-blooded deeds, the suppression of personal freedom, the brutal practice of slave labor, the depravities of the concentration camp, the massacre of his own followers in June 1934, the killing of war prisoners and the mass slaughter of the Jews. . . .

The blueprint of what the Almighty had called upon him to do in this cataclysmic world and the philosophy, the *Weltanschauung,* that would sustain it were set down in cold print [in *Mein Kampf*] for all to ponder. That philosophy, however demented, had roots, as we have seen, deep in German life. The blueprint may have seemed preposterous to most twentieth-century minds, even in Germany. But it too possessed a certain logic. It held forth a vision. It offered, though few saw this at the time, a continuation of German history. It pointed the way toward a glorious German destiny.

KLAUS EPSTEIN (1927–   ) was born in Germany and educated at Harvard University. He has lectured widely in German universities and is now professor of history at Brown. Author of the standard book on Matthias Erzberger, he is noted also for his perceptive commentaries on the work of other historians. The following selection is drawn from his highly critical review of Shirer's history of the Third Reich. At what specific points does Epstein's criticism seem most effective? What parts of Shirer's thesis seem best able to withstand attack? Why does Epstein emphasize the importance of the immediate historical setting of the Weimar Republic in studying Hitler's accession to power?*

Shirer's Argument Challenged

William Shirer's *Rise and Fall of the Third Reich: A History of Nazi Germany* (New York, 1960) has been widely hailed as a great work of history. Harry Schermann, chairman of the board of directors of the Book of the Month Club, says that it "will almost certainly come to be considered the definitive history of one of the most frightful chapters in the story of mankind." The book has already sold more widely than any work on European history published in recent years. It is probable that tens of thousands of American readers will take their views on recent German affairs from Shirer's pages for years to come. For that reason, it is important to point out the serious shortcomings of this work. . . .

Shirer presents his general interpretation of German history in a background chapter, "The Mind of Hitler and the Roots of the Third Reich." He is convinced that there is a specific logic which governs the course of German development and that he possesses the key to that logic. German history from 1871 to 1945 runs "in a straight line and with utter logic." Nazism is "but a logical continuation of German history." He frequently talks about the German national character, which he believes to have been shaped by such miscellaneous factors as the long experience of disunity, a penchant for sadism (and masochism), and Germany's general backwardness. Some of his judgments in connection with the latter point reveal much igno-

* From Klaus Epstein, "Shirer's History of Nazi Germany" in *Review of Politics*, vol. 23, no. 2 (April, 1961), pp. 230–245. Reprinted by permission of Review of Politics.

rance and prejudice. Shirer states, for example, that Germany was reduced, after the Peace of Westphalia in 1648, "to the barbarism of Muscovy." But where is the Russian Leibnitz of the next generation? Shirer's view of the Hohenzollerns is as follows: "Under Brandenburg's ruling princes, the Hohenzollerns, who were little more than military adventurers, the Slavs, mostly Poles, were gradually pushed back along the Baltic." This statement is mistaken on several grounds. Anybody possessing the slightest familiarity with German medieval history knows that the *Drang nach Osten,* which gradually pushed the Slavs back along the Baltic, was completed well before 1400, whereas the Hohenzollerns became margraves of Brandenburg only in 1417. To refer to the Hohenzollerns as "little more than military adventurers" does little credit to Shirer's knowledge of Prussian history. Frederick I (1417–40), was one of the greatest German princes of the fifteenth century. Joachim I (1499–1535) founded the University of Frankfurt and was instrumental in the reception of Roman Law. Joachim II (1535–71) introduced the Reformation and reorganized the entire administrative structure of his state. The Great Elector (1640–88) was one of the most versatile rulers of his age, a vigorous mercantilist, a patron of culture, and a great administrator, in short the very antithesis of a military adventurer. I will charitably assume that Shirer's statement was intended to apply only to the early Hohenzollerns—it is even more patently absurd when applied to Frederick I, Frederick William I, Frederick the Great, etc. Shirer's ignorance about Prussia is complemented by strong prejudices on that subject—leading him to general accusations which include statements such as that "even Kant preached that

duty demands the suppression of human feeling . . ." Did Socrates in fact teach anything else?

Shirer's judgment on the German state which Bismarck created is as follows: "a problem child of Europe and the world for nearly a century, a nation of gifted, vigorous people in which first this remarkable man [Bismarck] and then Kaiser Wilhelm and finally Hitler, aided by a military caste and by many a strange intellectual, succeeded in inculcating a lust for power and domination, a passion for unbridled militarism, a contempt for democracy and individual freedom and a longing for authority, for authoritarianism. . . ."

Can this be considered a balanced judgment? Shirer accuses not only the German middle class but also the working class of trading "for material gain any aspirations for political freedom they may have had," with Bismarck's social legislation having "a profound influence on the working class in that it gradually made them value security over political freedom and caused them to see in the State, however conservative, a benefactor and a protector." Bismarck himself would have been most surprised by this indirect compliment to a policy which is generally held to have been a failure. Another sweeping thought-killing generalization is the following: "They [the German middle class] accepted the Hohenzollern autocracy. They *gladly* knuckled under to the Junker bureaucracy and they *fervently* embraced Prussian militarism. Germany's star had risen and they—almost all the people—were *eager* to do what their masters asked to keep it high" [my italics]. One can only ask: did the readers of the *Frankfurter Zeitung,* Germany's great liberal newspaper, belong to this kind of a homogeneous middle class? Shirer obviously does not have the slightest idea of the extent and vigor of the criticism which Left Liberals and Socialists continually delivered against the ruling group, military and civilian, of Wilhelmian Germany. He might profitably study the *Reichstag* debates on the *Daily Telegraph* (November, 1908) or the Saverne Incidents (December, 1913)—to mention only two examples—to correct his unbalanced view of German prewar political life.

Shirer's one-sided misjudgments on Germany's political history appear relatively insignificant when compared with his systematic prejudice when dealing with Germany's cultural heritage. Hitler's *Weltanschauung* "has its roots deep in German history and thought," more specifically in "that odd assortment of erudite but unbalanced philosophers, historians and teachers who captured the German mind during the century before Hitler." Shirer traces the pedigree of Nazism back to Fichte (described as delivering his nationalist Addresses "from the podium of the University of Berlin" in 1807,[1] Hegel (because he glorified the state and the hero), Treitschke (because he preached Prussianism and war), Nietzsche (because he gloried in elitism and expressed contempt for Christianity), and Wagner (whose world of "the barbaric, pagan Nibelungs . . . has always fascinated the German mind and answered some terrible longing in the German soul"). Shirer adds Gobineau and Houston S. Chamberlain to this list of the precursors of Nazism while regretting that "the limitations of space in a work of this kind prohibited discussion of the considerable influence on the Third Reich of a number of other German intellectuals whose writings were popular and significant in Ger-

many: Schlegel, J. Goerres, Novalis, Arndt, Jahn, Lagarde, List, Droysen, Ranke, Mommsen, Constantin Frantz, Stöcker, Bernhardi, Klaus Wagner, Langbehn, Lange, Spengler." This grab-bag miscellany of names is unlikely to give the informed reader a favorable view of Shirer's mastery of German intellectual history. Shirer documents his one-sided theme by presenting parallel passages from Hitler, Hegel, and Nietzsche. It is superfluous to comment on this crude throwback to wartime pamphleteering. Shirer falls into every one of the frequently exposed fallacies of his predecessors in the field of Nazi pedigree-hunting (McGovern, Viereck, Rohan O'Butler, etc.) : (1) exaggerating the specificity of the influence exercised by any so-called precursor; (2) extracting from the works of any so-called precursor those quotations which in some way anticipate Nazism, even though they may be a relatively unimportant element in the total corpus of an author's thought; (3) identifying Germany's intellectual heritage with a line of selected precursors, while ignoring those figures—however important in their own age (for example, Goethe)—who do not fit into such a pedigree; (4) ignoring "proto-Nazi thinkers" in non-German lands (for example, Carlyle or Danilevsky) whose existence throws considerable doubt upon a German uniqueness in this respect. The result of Shirer's kind of history is a garbled *ad hoc* presentation of the German heritage drawn up to prove what is clearly an *a priori* case. . . .

The trouble with this kind of approach is not only that it distorts history, but it prevents a man who believes in it from asking many important questions about Nazism. Shirer never asks why there was so little popular resistance to the Nazi accession to power in 1933.

---

[1] It may be noted in passing that the University of Berlin, as any student of the Prussian Reform period knows, was founded only in 1810.

He simply does not recognize this as a problem, for the entire German heritage made it inevitable—in his view—that Germans should greet Nazism enthusiastically. He does not ask: What went wrong with the German Socialists, once formidable and courageous champions of liberty? Or the Zentrum which had resisted Bismarck so heroically? Or the liberal section of the bourgeoisie, which had rallied to the Republic in 1918? The reader will vainly look in Shirer's book for answers to these problems. The chapters dealing with the period of the Weimar Republic—and especially its collapse—are nothing but a conventional chronicle unaccompanied by analysis. Shirer frequently provides denunciation where explanation is called for. Take, for example, his well-justified attack upon the conduct of the German Conservatives from 1930–1933. "With a narrowness, a prejudice, a blindness, which in retrospect seem inconceivable to this chronicler, they hammered away at the foundations of the Republic." Is it too much to expect that a historian of the Third Reich should seek to explain this Conservative obtusensss, so essential a factor in Hitler's attainment of power. Shirer has completely ignored the excellent recent German studies which explain in minute detail how the "inconceivable" actually happened.

Lack of analysis is not the only weakness which besets Shirer's chapters dealing with Weimar. He is very weak in portraying the general mood of despair which characterized the early years of the Republic, or the specific Bavarian milieu in which Nazism was born. . . . These points, representative of many half-true, mistaken, or prejudiced judgments that could be mentioned, indicate that Shirer's background knowledge of German political and intellectual history does not equip him to place Nazism in the general stream of Germany's development. . . .

It is clear, I trust, from this critical essay that a profound and balanced history of Nazi Germany remains to be written. It must avoid Shirer's rewarming of the wartime tale that German history is a one-way road leading from Luther to Hitler. It must seek to understand Nazism in the general context of modern totalitarianism. It must seek to ascertain the specific pattern of causation—including national character and historic legacies, but also the concrete circumstances, national and international—which led to the Nazi triumph in Germany in 1933. It must strive for a balance between diplomatic, political, social, economic, institutional and cultural history. It must be abreast of current scholarship, especially the very fruitful research conducted in Germany today. It must seek answers to the right kinds of questions instead of being satisfied with a mere chronicle of events. It should be animated, above all, by a generous and large-minded temper which conquers prejudice and allows the historian to comprehend not only Nazi criminals and accomplices, but also heroic resistants, in giving a total portrait of Germany in the Nazi era.

A. J. P. TAYLOR (1906–   ), one of the most
provocative historians writing today, is a Fellow
of Magdalen College, Oxford, and widely known in
Britain as a lecturer, journalist, and commentator
on BBC. He has written many books and essays
on recent German history; all of them present
challenging interpretations. His delight in taking
issue with the conclusions of others is suggested
in the following explanation of Hitler's rise to
power. Taylor avoids Shirer's argument that
Nazism was the result of German history and,
following Epstein's advice, looks to the immediate
setting in the Weimar Republic for the causes
of Hitlerism. In so doing, he discounts both
emphasis on Hitler's personality and the explanation
that Hitler's success was due primarily to
social-psychological conditions in postwar Germany.
Political factors alone, Taylor concludes, are
sufficient to explain the coming of the Nazis.*

The Result of Political Intrigue

National-Socialism was based on fraud;
and no fraud was greater than the legend
of the seizure of power, which was supposed to have taken place on 30th January 1933. Certainly this day, on which
Hitler became Chancellor, was the most
important moment in his life and a
turning-point in German history. But
there was no seizure of power. That had
been tried by Hitler at Munich in November 1923. It had failed; and he was
determined never to repeat the attempt.
There was an alternative path to power
which he sometimes contemplated: that
the Nazi Party should actually win a
majority of the popular vote and thus
impose Hitler as Chancellor by strict
democratic choice. But this alternative,
too, proved beyond him. The Nazis
never received more than 37 per cent of
votes at a free election for the *Reichstag.*
The third path, and that which Hitler
followed, was the way of intrigue; he
would become Chancellor as the leader
of a minority and would then use the
power of the State to establish his dictatorship. The answer to the question
how Hitler came to power is therefore
to be found more in the actions of those
German politicians who were not National-Socialists than in those of Hitler
himself. He waited; they decided.

* From "The Seizure of Power" by A. J. P. Taylor in Maurice Baumont, John H. E. Fried, and
Edmond Vermeil (eds.), *The Third Reich,* published under the auspices of the International Council
for Philosophy and Humanistic Studies and with the assistance of UNESCO (New York, 1955),
pp. 523–526, 533–535.

The Weimar Republic always suffered from a multiplicity of parties. No single party ever possessed a majority in the *Reichstag;* and every German government after 1918 rested on a coalition. This would have mattered less if there had been at least a majority in favour of the Republic; but this, too, was lacking after the first elections in 1919. The middle-class Liberal parties faded and disappeared. Only the Social Democrats remained a genuine Weimar party. The Nationalists welcomed anything that weakened the Republic; the Communists welcomed anything that discredited the Social Democrats. The Roman Catholic Centre Party certainly took part in republican governments along with the Social Democrats; but it had no republican principles. It was a sectarian party, ready to work with any system that would protect Roman Catholic interests; and in the last days of the Republic it stretched out its hand to the forces of destruction, just as in the last days of the Empire it had turned to the republicans. Every party contributed to the fall of the Weimar Republic—the Social Democrats from timidity, the others with conscious ill-will. But none contributed with such cynicism as the Centre—indifferent to the Republic or even to Germany, so long as the Roman Catholic schools enjoyed their favoured position.

The failure to establish strong stable governments brought unexpected power to the President. The makers of the constitution in 1919 had intended to give him the position of monarch in a parliamentary State choosing the Chancellor, but without independent authority in himself. The Chancellor was to be the heir of Bismarck, the true wielder of power. But the short-lived Chancellors never held this position. They were little more than parliamentary managers for the President. Even Ebert drew on his

reserve of authority. Hindenburg, who became President in 1925, possessed it in greater measure and believed that his duty was to use it. Moreover, as the military leader of the World War, Hindenburg both commanded the allegiance of the army and voiced its demands. The army was the one stable point of order in an unstable society. It is a mistake to suggest, as some have done, that the army chiefs were bent on overthrowing the Republic. They would have attempted this only if the republican politicians had accepted permanently and sincerely the disarmament imposed upon Germany by the Treaty of Versailles; and none did so. The generals were willing to work with the Republic if it provided stable government. But this it failed to do. . . .

This, then, is the background of Hitler's rise to power. Far from his hammering at a door which was long kept closed against him, he was constantly being invited to enter by those within; and he held back in order to increase his market value. Everyone assumed that he would end up as Chancellor sooner or later. The real problem in German history is why so few of the educated, civilised classes recognised Hitler as the embodiment of evil. University professors; army officers; businessmen and bankers—these had a background of culture, and even of respect for law. Yet virtually none of them exclaimed: 'This is anti-Christ.' Later, they were to make out that Hitler had deceived them and that the bestial nature of National-Socialism could not have been foreseen. This is not true. The real character of National-Socialism was exposed by many foreign, and even by some German, observers long before Hitler came to power. It could be judged from Hitler's writings and his speeches; it was displayed in every street brawl that the Nazi Brown Shirts organised. Hitler did not deceive the responsible classes in Germany: they deceived themselves. Their self-deception had a simple cause: they were engaged in fighting the wrong battle and in saving Germany from the wrong enemy. Hitler's hostility to Communism was his strongest asset. The Bolshevik peril in Germany had once perhaps been real; therefore anyone who was anti-Communist seemed to be on the side of civilisation, and the Communists themselves fed this illusion by treating Hitler as their only serious enemy. 'Better Hitler than Communism' was the phrase which opened the way for Hitler first within Germany and then on a wider scale in Europe. . . .

Even so, the lack of alarm among civilised Germans remains a strange puzzle. The explanation may perhaps be found in the taste which so many of them had for political intrigue. A country with a long constitutional history develops a political class. The politicians look after government. The generals and bankers and professors mind their own business. This has always been true in England; and it was largely true in the third French republic, despite an occasional political general. In Germany men were always coming in from outside; a political class never had a chance to develop. Even Bismarck was a gifted amateur, who knew nothing of politics until he started at the top. Of his successors as Imperial Chancellor, one was a general, one a diplomatist, one a civil servant. In the reign of Wilhelm II generals like Waldersee and Ludendorff pushed into politics on one side; and business-men like Ballin or Rathenau pushed in on the other. The practice was maintained in the Weimar Republic. There was no true statesman in Germany after the death of Strese-mann in 1929. Her fate was in the hands of amateurs, who mistook intrigue for political activity. Hindenburg, the President, was a retired professional soldier, a Field-Marshal over eighty years old. Brüning, who became Chancellor in 1930, was half scholar, half army captain, but never strictly a party leader. Papen, his successor, was a dashing cavalry-man of great wealth, with no political standing. Schleicher, the most influential of all, lived for intrigue and nothing else: claiming to represent army opinion with the President and the President's authority to the army, but in fact playing off one against the other. All four thought that they were a great deal cleverer than Hitler and that they would take him prisoner in no time. . . .

On 30th January Hitler became Chancellor. This was far from a seizure of power. Indeed, the forces of the old order imagined that they had seized Hitler. Though he was Chancellor, there were only three Nazis in a Cabinet of eleven; the two key posts of Foreign Minister and Minister of Defence were in the hands of non-political agents of the President; and Hitler could not see Hindenburg except in the presence of Papen, who was Vice-Chancellor. No arrangement could have been neater or more cynical. Yet it broke down within the first few days. What Hitler appreciated and his conservative associates did not was that, while the Nazi Party was not strong enough to seize power when the forces of the State were hostile, it was strong enough to do so once these forces were neutral or on its side. . . . Hitler supposed that he could indeed deliver the parliamentary majority which had hitherto evaded everybody. Once the National-Socialists dominated the *Reichstag*, he could shake off Papen and the other elderly gentlemen who controlled him, and establish a Nazi dictatorship by law.

Hitler's calculation did not succeed. The election campaign was conducted with every weapon of Nazi terror; and the burning of the *Reichstag* building on 27th February enabled Hitler to declare the Communist Party illegal. Nevertheless on 5th March the National-Socialists secured only 43.9 per cent of the votes. Even with the co-operation of the right-wing Nationalists they had only a bare majority—enough to control the *Reichstag* from day to day, but not enough to carry through any fundamental change in the constitution. Hitler, however, was set on an Enabling Law which would give him all the powers of a dictator. If the so-called democratic parties had held together, Hitler would have been driven to illegal action—or would have remained powerless. The Communists had been driven underground. The Social Democrats, though feeble in action, held nobly to their principles and voted against the Enabling Law, despite the threats of terror against them. The decision rested on the Centre, with its 102 votes. The leaders of the Centre were men of personal courage. But their Party cared little for democracy; it was concerned only to secure the position of the Roman Catholic schools. It had a long tradition of doing this by intriguing with successive parties and governments; it had long lost the tradition of resistance which had once enabled it to defeat Bismarck. The Centre leaders were fobbed off with promises from Hitler in which they only half believed; and on 23rd March the Centre votes were cast in favour of the Enabling Law. These votes alone gave Hitler's dictatorship its legal character.

If we look back over this wretched story, we see a man bent on success on the one side, and a group of politicians without ideas or principles on the other. Hitler was resolved to gain power. He did not know how he would do it, and he tried many means which failed; but he had an unbreakable purpose. The others were only concerned to strike a bargain with him. If there had been a strong democratic sentiment in Germany, Hitler would never have come to power—or even to prominence. He would have failed even if the weak democratic parties had held together. He had two great weapons. He could promise the generals a great army, if they let him in; he could threaten civil disturbance, if they kept him out. The promise was more potent than the threat. One can blame all the parties in turn. The Communists started the habit of violence and disrupted the working-class front. The Social Democrats had lost all ability to act and faith in their strength. The Centre would bargain with anybody, even with Hitler. But the greatest responsibility lay with those who let Hitler in and established him as Chancellor. Hitler recognised it himself. In 1938 Papen, then German ambassador at Vienna, accompanied Schuschnigg to the fateful interview at Berchtesgaden which ended Austrian independence. In the course of the argument, Hitler turned to Papen and said: 'By making me Chancellor, Herr von Papen, you made possible the National-Socialist revolution in Germany. I shall never forget it.' And Papen answered with soldierly pride: 'Certainly, my *Führer.*'

Until he was forced to flee his native Germany in 1936, FRANZ NEUMANN (1900–1954) had been an economist and lawyer for the German trade union movement. During World War II he served as chief of the German Research Section of the American OSS. He later became professor of government at Columbia University. The following selection is taken from his analysis of the structure and practice of National Socialism, an early study which must still be considered one of the most important books on Nazi Germany. Neumann here gives a Marxian explanation for the rise of Hitler. In what ways does this interpretation complement and support Taylor's thesis? In what important respect does Neumann differ from Fromm in assessing Hitler's mass appeal to the German people? *

The Conspiracy of Monopoly Capitalists

The thesis of this article is that the National Socialist Revolution is a counter-revolution of a monopolized industry and the big landowners against democracy and social progress; that this revolution was only successful because the structure and practice of the Weimar Constitution facilitated it; and . . . that the Social Democratic party and the German free trade unions which were the sole defenders of parliamentary democracy were too weak to fight against National Socialism. . . .[1]

[The Social Democratic Party and the trade unions] alone in post-war Ger-

many could have swung the great masses of the people over to democracy; not only the workers but also the middle classes, the section of the population that suffered most from the process of monopolization.

Other strata reacted to the complex post-war and post-revolution situation exactly as one would have expected. The big estate owners pursued a reactionary policy in every field. Monopolistic industry hated and fought the trade unions and the political system that gave the unions their status. The army used every available means to strengthen chauvinistic nationalism in order to restore itself to its former greatness. The judiciary invariably sided with the right and the civil services supported counter-revolu-

[1] The first sentence of this selection comes from Franz Neumann, "The Decay of German Democracy" in *The Political Quarterly*, vol. IV, no. 4 (1933) p. 256.

* From Franz Neumann, *Behemoth: The Structure and Practice of National Socialism* (New York, 1944), pp. 13–16; 20–23; 29–30; 33–34. Reprinted by permission of Mrs. Inge S. Marcuse.

tionary movements. Yet the Social Democracy was unable to organize either the whole of the working class or the middle classes. It lost sections of the former and never won a real foothold with the latter. The Social Democrats lacked a consistent theory, competent leadership, and freedom of action. Unwittingly, they strengthened the monopolistic trends in German industry, and, placing complete reliance on formalistic legality, they were unable to root out the reactionary elements in the judiciary and civil service or limit the army to its proper constitutional role.

The strong man of the Social Democratic party, Otto Braun, Prussian prime minister until 20 June 1932 when he was deposed by the Hindenburg-Papen coup d'état, attributes the failure of the party and Hitler's successful seizure of power to a combination of Versailles and Moscow. This defense is neither accurate nor particularly skilful. The Versailles Treaty naturally furnished excellent propaganda material against democracy in general and against the Social Democratic party in particular, and the Communist party unquestionably made inroads among Social Democrats. Neither was primarily responsible for the fall of the Republic, however. Besides, what if Versailles and Moscow had been the two major factors in the making of National Socialism? Would it not have been the task of a great democratic leadership to make the democracy work in spite of and against Moscow and Versailles? That the Social Democratic party failed remains the crucial fact, regardless of any official explanation. It failed because it did not see that the central problem was the imperialism of Germany monopoly capital, becoming ever more urgent with the continued growth of the process of monopolization. The more monopoly grew, the more incompatible it became with the political democracy. . . .

The efficient and powerfully organized German system of our time was born under the stimulus of a series of factors brought into the forefront by the First World War. The inflation of the early '20s permitted unscrupulous entrepreneurs to build up giant economic empires at the expense of the middle and working classes. The prototype was the Stinnes empire and it is at least symbolic that Hugo Stinnes was the most inveterate enemy of democracy and of Rathenau's foreign policy. Foreign loans that flowed into Germany after 1924 gave Germany industry the liquid capital needed to rationalize and enlarge their plants. . . . Trusts, combines, and cartels covered the whole economy with a network of authoritarian organizations. Employers' organizations controlled the labor market, and big business lobbies aimed at placing the legislative, administrative, and judicial machinery at the service of monopoly capital.

In Germany there was never anything like the popular anti-monopoly movement of the United States under Theodore Roosevelt and Woodrow Wilson. Industry and finance were of course firmly convinced that the cartel and trust represented the highest forms of economic organization. The independent middle class was not articulate in its opposition, except against department stores and chains. Though the middle class belonged to powerful pressure groups, like the Federal Union of German Industries, big business leaders were invariably their spokesmen.

Labor was not at all hostile to the process of trustification. The Communists regarded monopoly as an inevitable stage in the development of capitalism and hence considered it futile to fight capital concentration rather than the system itself. Ironically enough, the policy of the reformist wing of the labor movement was not significantly different in effect. The Social Democrats and the trade unions also regarded concentration as inevitable, and, they added, as a higher form of capitalist organization. . . .

The largest trusts in German history were formed during the Weimar Republic. The merger in 1926 of four large steel companies in western Germany resulted in the formation of the *Vereinigte Stahlwerke* (the United Steel Works). The *Vereinigte Oberschlesische Hüttenwerke* (the United Upper Silesian Mills) was a similar combination among the steel industries of Upper Silesia. The *I. G. Farbenindustrie* (the German Dye Trust) arose in 1925 through the merger of the six largest corporations in this field, all of which had previously been combined in a pool. In 1930 the capital stock of the Dye Trust totaled 1,100,000,-000 marks and the number of workers it employed reached 100,000. . . .

In the center of the counter-revolution stood the judiciary. Unlike administrative acts, which rest on consideration of convenience and expediency, judicial decisions rest on law, that is on right and wrong, and they always enjoy the limelight of publicity. Law is perhaps the most pernicious of all weapons in political struggles, precisely because of the halo that surrounds the concepts of right and justice. 'Right,' Hocking has said, 'is psychologically a claim whose infringement is met with a resentment deeper than the injury would satisfy, a resentment that may amount to passion for which men will risk life and property as they would never do for an expediency.' When it becomes 'political,' justice breeds hatred and despair among those it singles out for attack. Those whom it favors, on the other hand, develop a profound con-tempt for the very value of justice; they know that it can be purchased by the powerful. As a device for strengthening one political group at the expense of others, for eliminating enemies and assisting political allies, law then threatens the fundamental convictions upon which the tradition of our civilization rests.

The technical possibilities of perverting justice for political ends are widespread in every legal system; in republican Germany, they were as numerous as the paragraphs of the penal code. Perhaps the chief reason lay in the very nature of criminal trials, for, unlike the American system, the proceedings were dominated not by counsel but by the presiding judge. The power of the judge, furthermore, was strengthened year after year. . . . A comparative analysis of three *causes célèbres* will make it amply clear that the Weimar criminal courts were part and parcel of the anti-democratic camp.

After the downfall of the Bavarian Soviet Republic in 1919, the courts handed down the following sentences:

> 407 persons, fortress imprisonment
> 1737 persons, prison
> 65 persons, imprisoned at hard labor

Every adherent of the Soviet Republic who had the slightest connection with the unsuccessful coup was sentenced.

The contrast with the judicial treatment of the 1920 right-wing Kapp Putsch could not possibly have been more complete. Fifteen months after the putsch, the Reich ministry of justice announced officially on 21 May 1921 that a total of 705 charges of high treason had been examined. Of them,

> 412 in the opinion of the courts came under the amnesty law of 4 August 1920, despite the fact that the

statute specifically excluded the putsch leaders from its provisions

108 had become obsolete because of death or other reasons

174 were not pressed

11 were unfinished

Not one person had been punished. Nor did the statistics give the full picture. Of the eleven cases pending on 21 May 1921, only one ended in a sentence; former Police President von Jagow of Berlin received five years' honorary confinement. When the Prussian state withdrew Jagow's pension, the federal supreme court ordered it restored to him. The guiding spirit of the putsch, Dr. Kapp, died before trial. Of the other leaders, some like General von Lüttwitz and Majors Papst and Bischoff escaped; General Ludendorff was not prosecuted because the court chose to accept his alibi that he was present only by accident; General von Lettow-Vorbeck, who had occupied a whole town for Kapp, was declared to have been not a leader but merely a follower.

The third significant illustration is the judicial handling of Hitler's abortive Munich putsch of 1923. Hitler, Pöhner, Kriebel, and Weber received five years; Röhm, Frick, Brückner, Pernet, and Wagner one year and three months. Ludendorff once again was present only by accident and was released. Although section 9 of the Law for the Protection of the Republic clearly and unmistakably ordered the deportation of every alien convicted of high treason, the Munich People's Court exempted Hitler on the specious argument that, despite his Austrian citizenship, he considered himself a German.

It would be futile to relate in detail the history of political justice under the Weimar Republic. A few more illus-trations will suffice. The penal code created the crime of 'treason to the country' to cover the betrayal of military and other secrets to foreign agents. The courts, however, promptly found a special political use for these provisions. After the Versailles Treaty forced Germany to disarm, the Reichswehr encouraged the formation of secret and illegal bodies of troops, the so-called 'black Reichswehr.' When liberals, pacifists, socialists, and communists denounced this violation of both international obligations and German law (for the treaty had become part of the German legal system), they were arrested and tried for treason to the country committed through the press. Thus did the courts protect the illegal and reactionary black Reichswehr. Assassinations perpetrated by the black Reichswehr against alleged traitors within their ranks (the notorious Fehme murders), on the other hand, were either not prosecuted at all or were dealt with lightly. . . .

It is impossible to escape the conclusion that political justice is the blackest page in the life of the German Republic. The judicial weapon was used by the reaction with steadily increasing intensity. . . .

The Social Democracy and the trade unions were completely helpless against the many-sided attacks on the Weimar democracy. Moderate attempts were made to spread the idea of an economic democracy, but this new ideology proved even less attractive than the old Socialist program. Salaried employees remained aloof; the civil-service organization affiliated with the Socialist trade unions declined in membership from 420,000 in 1922 to 172,000 in 1930, while the so-called neutral, but in fact Nationalistic, civil-service body organized 1,043,-000 members in 1930, primarily from the middle and lower ranks. The significance of these figures is obvious.

The Social Democratic party was trapped in contradictions. Though it still claimed to be a Marxian party, its policy had long been one of pure gradualism. It never mustered the courage to drop one or the other, traditional ideology or reformist policy. A radical break with tradition and the abandonment of Marxism would have delivered thousands of adherents into the Communist camp. To have abandoned gradualism for a revolutionary policy, on the other hand, would have required cutting the many links binding the party to the existing state. The Socialists therefore retained this ambiguous position and they could not create a democratic consciousness. The Weimar constitution, attacked on the right by Nationalists, National Socialists, and reactionary liberals, and on the left by the Communists, remained merely a transitory phenomenon for the Social Democrats, a first step to a greater and better future. And a transitory scheme cannot arouse much enthusiasm.

Even before the beginning of the great depression, therefore, the ideological, economic, social, and political systems were no longer functioning properly. Whatever appearance of successful operation they may have given was based primarily on toleration by the antidemocratic forces and on the fictitious prosperity made possible by foreign loans. The depression uncovered and deepened the petrification of the traditional social and political structure. The social contracts on which that structure was founded broke down. The Democratic party disappeared; the Catholic Center shifted to the right; and the Social Democrats and Communists devoted far more energy to fighting each other than to the struggle against the growing threat of National Socialism. The National Socialist party in turn heaped abuse upon the Social Democrats. They coined the epithet, November Criminals: a party of corruptionists and pacifists responsible for the defeat in 1918, for the Versailles Treaty, for the inflation.

The output of German industry had dropped sharply. Unemployment was rising: six million were registered in January 1932, and there were perhaps two million more of the so-called invisible unemployed. Only a small fraction received unemployment insurance and an ever larger proportion received no support at all. The unemployed youth became a special problem in themselves. There were hundreds of thousands who had never held jobs. Unemployment became a status, and, in a society where success is paramount, a stigma. Peasants revolted in the north while large estate owners cried for financial assistance. Small businessmen and craftsmen faced destruction. Houseowners could not collect their rents. Banks crashed and were taken over by the federal government. Even the stronghold of industrial reaction, the United Steel Trust, was near collapse and its shares were purchased by the federal government at prices far above the market quotation. The budget situation became precarious. The reactionaries refused to support a large-scale works program lest it revive the declining power of the trade unions, whose funds were dwindling and whose membership was declining. . . .

Every social system must somehow satisfy the primary needs of the people. The imperial system succeeded to the extent and so long as it was able to expand. A successful policy of war and imperialist expansion had reconciled large sections of the population to the semi-absolutism. In the face of the material advantages gained, the anomalous character of the political structure was not decisive. The army, the bureaucracy, industry, and the big agrarians ruled. The divine-right theory—the official political doctrine—merely veiled their rule and it was not taken seriously. The imperial rule was in fact not absolutistic, for it was bound by law, proud of its *Rechtsstaat* theory. It lost out and abdicated when its expansionist policy was checked.

The Weimar democracy proceeded in a different direction. It had to rebuild an impoverished and exhausted country in which class antagonisms had become polarized. It attempted to merge three elements: the heritage of the past (especially the civil service), parliamentary democracy modeled after Western European and American patterns, and a pluralistic collectivism, the incorporation of the powerful social and economic organizations directly into the political system. What it actually produced, however, were sharpened social antagonisms, the breakdown of voluntary collaboration, the destruction of parliamentary institutions, the suspension of political liberties, the growth of a ruling bureaucracy, and the renaissance of the army as a decisive political factor.

Why?

In an impoverished, yet highly industrialized, country, pluralism could work only under the following different conditions. In the first place, it could rebuild Germany with foreign assistance, expanding its markets by peaceful means to the level of its high industrial capacity. The Weimar Republic's foreign policy tended in this direction. By joining the concert of the Western European powers the Weimar government hoped to obtain concessions. The attempt failed. It was supported neither by German industry and large landowners nor by the Western powers. The year 1932 found Germany in a catastrophic political, economic, and social crisis.

The system could also operate if the ruling groups made concessions voluntarily or under compulsion by the state. That would have led to a better life for the mass of the German workers and security for the middle classes at the expense of the profits and power of big business. German industry was decidedly not amenable, however, and the state sided with it more and more.

The third possibility was the transformation into a socialist state, and that had become completely unrealistic in 1932 since the Social Democratic party was socialist only in name.

The crisis of 1932 demonstrated that political democracy alone without a fuller utilization of the potentialities inherent in Germany's industrial system, that is, without the abolition of unemployment and an improvement in living standards, remained a hollow shell.

The fourth choice was the return to imperialist expansion. Imperialist ventures could not be organized within the traditional democratic form, however, for there would have been too serious an opposition. Nor could it take the form of restoration of the monarchy. An industrial society that has passed through a democratic phase cannot exclude the masses from consideration. Expansionism therefore took the form of National Socialism, a totalitarian dictatorship that has been able to transform some of its victims into supporters and to organize the entire country into an armed camp under iron discipline.

ZEVEDEI BARBU (1914–   ) was born in Rumania, has lectured at the University of Glasgow, and is now teaching at the University of Sussex in England. The book from which this selection is taken is a penetrating study of the social forces shaping various forms of government. Barbu maintains that the reason the Nazis came to power lies in the social and psychological conditions in Germany in 1933. On what issues does Barbu agree with Fromm? Where do they differ? What social classes, according to Barbu, contributed most to Hitler's success?*

The Product of
Social-Psychological Malaise

Most students of Nazism are inclined to look at the origins of this movement from a purely economic point of view. Lenin can be considered among the first who, from a Marxian viewpoint, foresaw a certain stage in the evolution of Western civilization which might be described as Fascism. The interests of various national economic systems will lead, according to Lenin, to an aggressive type of nationalism for which racial and nationalistic doctrines will be the most adequate ideological weapons. Basing his view on this thesis, Dr. F. Neumann writes: 'German National Socialism is nothing but the dictatorship of a monopolized industry and of the big estate owners, the nakedness of which is covered by the mask of a corporative state.'

Charles Bettelheim sees the core of Nazism in the aggressive policy of the magnates of German industry, who have in their hands 'tous les leviers de commande' [all the levers of power]. Often Nazism is called simply a 'dictatorship of monopoly capitalism.'

All these views imply that the structure of Nazism is closely related to the interests of the socially and economically upper strata of German Society. The main piece of evidence which is constantly produced by the supporters of this thesis is the fact that the Nazi movement was, particularly at its beginning, financed by many outstanding representatives of German industry. But today there is little doubt that this fact did not influence the structure of Hitler's

* Reprinted from *Democracy and Dictatorship: Their Psychology and Patterns of Life* by Zevedei Barbu, published by Grove Press, Inc. Copyright 1956 by Grove Press. Published in England by Routledge & Kegan Paul, Ltd. Pp. 121–122, 124–126, 128–130, 144–147.

movement, except in minor tactical points. In fact Hitler and his party could never be considered the 'puppets' of the German upper classes. L. von Mises obviously speaks the truth when saying that 'Thyssen and the rest paid him (Hitler), but they did not bribe him.' On the contrary, the party organization, its aims, and the attitudes of its members could hardly fit into the interests and way of life of these social strata. Even Nazi bellicosity has little in common with the aggressive expansionistic attitude of the German industrialists. . . . The two types of aggression are widely different in their sources and modes of manifestation.

Another opinion, also widespread, is that Nazism was a lower-middle-class movement. . . . It is on this sociological view that Erich Fromm bases his psychological interpretation of Nazism. The main mental traits of the Nazi group, embodied in his concept of 'authoritarian character,' are characteristic features of the lower-middle classes. This point will be taken up at a later stage. For the moment it is enough to say that the statistical evidence on which this thesis is based is not conclusive. The membership list of 1935 shows the following figures: 32 per cent manual workers; 20.6 per cent, white collar employees; 20.2 per cent, independents; 13 per cent, officials; 10 per cent peasants; 3.4 per cent, others. The figures seem to show a certain preponderance of the middle-class element. But the point is that categories such as white collar employees, independents and officials can only arbitrarily be considered as together forming a social class. This type of approach to Nazism suffers from the ambiguity inherent in concepts such as the middle class, the lower-middle class, or petty bourgeoisie, which are often applicable only in very general terms. Many individuals who are believed to belong to these classes are in fact in a transitory state socially, and as such, they can better be described as classless. As will be seen later, classless individuals and groups have special significance for the structure of Nazism.

In conclusion we cannot see in the class approach to Nazism more than a comfortable hypothesis. As such it served the theoretical outlook of those intellectuals whose minds were tinted with an economistic or Marxian way of thinking. Any realistic approach to Nazism should, in our opinion, start by considering it as the outcome of an ethnic group—the German nation—living under conditions of stress caused by specific historical circumstances. . . .

During the period of the rise of Nazism the German nation lived in unique conditions of stress and insecurity. The defeat of 1918 is usually mentioned as the starting point in the development of this situation. Quick structural changes such as the downfall of the monarchy, the collapse of the army, the appearance of new political parties are also important contributing factors.[1] A series of inner contradictions and tensions within German society in the post-war period are in our opinion more important than the defeat itself, or the downfall of the Empire, for the understanding of this specific condition of stress and insecurity. Many demobilized soldiers and dismissed officers refused to go home and integrate themselves with the new conditions of life.

[1] Sometimes too much stress is laid on these general factors. The Kaiser, for instance, is often considered as the symbol of authority and security in pre-war Germany. His abdication was therefore bound to result in a deep crisis of authority which affected the position of every German father in his family. This caused a strong need for authority which drove the German youth into Hitler's hands.

They formed special military organizations, *Freikorps,* offering their protection to peasants threatened by raids of starving townsfolk, and to landlords from the eastern territories. And though the early Weimar régime used them in its struggle against the Communists, they became a menace to authority and security in the state by their independence and mercenary spirit. But, apart from the activities of the *Freikorps,* there were many other sources of instability and insecurity in the Weimar Republic. The Social Democrats were confused. Their manoeuvres between a strong Communist movement, deeply rooted in the German working classes, and the anti-Communist feelings of other classes and of the army in particular, resulted in a complete lack of orientation and of a programme. In this way, an inefficient government increased even more the frustration of the population. To this should be added a series of revolutionary attempts and Communist uprisings. Thus, the whole social atmosphere was loaded with tension, anxiety, and a spirit of brutality. The political parties took on a military character, each of them possessing fighting organizations.

The frustrating effects of economic crises, of unemployment, and particularly of the inflations of 1924 and 1929 are so well known that there is no need to enter into details. A word should be said about the contribution of the international scene to the situation of stress of the German group. Loss of colonies and national territories, military occupation, the reparation payments, and finally the French military occupation of the Ruhr district all intensified the insecurity. To all of this should be added the tensions caused in Bavaria—the birthplace of Nazism—by a series of separatist movements.

What are the most important psy-chological effects of this exceptional situation of stress? Perhaps the loss of the frame of reference for the behaviour of both group and individual is the most comprehensive symptom of this. The collapse of old institutions followed by a relatively long period of instability weakened and destroyed in many individuals the sense of discrimination and orientation in social life in particular. Since nothing remained unshaken, and certainly nothing unshakable, people swung from a state of naivety to one of desperate incredulity. All opinions were equally good, or all equally meaningless. They lived in a *Meinungschaos* [chaos of conflicting opinions] which produced in them apathy and complete detachment, and at the same time anxiety and readiness to do something, to do anything.

This state of mind affected, consciously or unconsciously, most individual members of German society. But the main problem for the social psychologist as well as for the political scientist is not the extension of this state of mind, but rather why a movement of the Right, Hitler's movement, presented itself as the best answer to it. Why could not Socialism or Communism play this role, for both exploited the feelings of frustration and insecurity in the masses, and both promised a stable social order? The answer to these questions is, in essence, simple. The Nazis offered to the people the quickest and the most radical way of relief from a situation of stress and insecurity. While the Socialists kept on talking vaguely in the name of peace and democracy, while the Communists promised a narrow class policy, the Nazis attacked the Versailles Treaty, promised economic autarky and employment. While the Socialists tied up the destiny of Germany with that of European democracy, and the Communists with that of Soviet Russia, the Nazis stirred up the feeling of pride of a heroic nation which is not only the master of its own destiny, but is called upon to master the world.

In principle there could be no competition with this kind of language addressed to a group in a condition of stress. It gave immediate outlets for the feeling of guilt and for the need of aggression, and provided a solution to the need for security in the near future. The Socialists and Communists were doomed to failure since the Nazis provided for the deeper and more immediate needs of the masses. They spoke about dignity to the humiliated, about power to the defeated, about the organic stability of human society to people who were experiencing the ruin and disintegration of age-old institutions. The society they spoke of was not an idea, and not of the future, as was that propounded by the Communists, but of the past, of the glorious German past. . . .

There was a bit of everything in the Nazi economic order. With the middle classes and peasantry the Nazis entertained their prejudices against Communism and their respect for private ownership. From this point of view one can say that the Nazis tried to please everybody. That is why it is hard to maintain that the movement had a class character. Though our reasons are different we nevertheless agree with von Mises when he writes: 'The German entrepreneurs and businessmen contributed their share to the triumph of Nazism, but so did all other strata of the nation.' In the following section we shall see who were the first and most reliable people to form the movement.

It would be true to say that, sociologically, Nazism, as a political and spiritual movement, represents a cross-section of the German nation during the inter-war period. It answered a state of frustration and insecurity widespread in all strata of the population during this period. It would also be right to infer from this that the cadres, and particularly the leadership of the party, were made up of individuals and groups who suffered more than others from frustration and insecurity.

The core of the party was formed by socially nondescript people, frustrated in their efforts to achieve a certain status in their society, the prototype of whom is Hitler. The demobilized soldiers and officers, former members of the *Freikorps,* formed an important Nazi group. Goering and Röhm are typical. Unemployed youngsters, émigrés, and students also found a point of attraction in the movement. To this is added a number of intellectuals frustrated in their aspirations, as Goebbels was, or incapable of adjusting themselves to the cultural climate of their time and consequently escaping into the mythical world of the past, like those belonging to the Thule Society of Munich. From the historically constituted classes Nazism attracted in the first place the peripheral elements. From the working class it attracted 'the flotsam, the strugglers living on the fringe of their own class, the workers of odd jobs, and the unemployed.' In the upper classes the party appealed in particular to aristocrats who identified themselves with a highly inadequate concept of their own class; they joined the party in order to re-make the position once held by the Junkers in Imperial Germany. Peasants who were by their aspirations above their group, or by their poverty below it, were also attracted to the movement.

All the individuals and groups mentioned above have one trait in common: they all can be called *déclassés,* that is, people who failed completely or partly to integrate themselves with one of the institutionalized forms of their society. They also suffer from lack of social attachment. In this way the *déclassés* can, by analogy with psychopathic personality, be described as sociopathic personalities. As the psychopathics are liable to all forms of delinquency, so are the sociopathics liable to political delinquency in particular, that is, they are breakers of the political order of their own society. . . .

The Nazi movement can be considered as the meeting point of all individuals and groups with an unstable social status; it evolved as a result of the disrupting processes taking place in the post-war period. It is, therefore, the classless element, rather than a particular social class, that should first be considered in order to understand Nazism. As opposed to any socialist party—obviously a class party—and to any democratic party normally based on a particular social group, Nazism represents in its structure the entire nation on a reduced scale. This is one of the first factors determining its totalitarian character.

Few psychologists interested in the origins of Nazism could escape the temptation of using the concept of national character. Most of them deal at large with the 'famous' and 'perennial' Germanic aggression, with the Germanic mysticism, ethnocentrism, authoritarian family, etc. Though far from expressing a definite opinion on this point, we feel that the concept of the national character is too much of a theoretical construct. Examples of aggression, collective or individual, can easily be found in every nation. Consequently we started to trace the origins of Nazism in a collective state of mind historically limited to the inter-war period. This is the state of mind created in a group of individuals under conditions of stress. A rigid social organization, certain mystical inclinations, group-centrism and aggression are normally involved in the behaviour of a group living under such conditions. To us the problem of the German national character is secondary as a determining factor in the rise of Nazism. . . .

The springboard of regression is the insecurity created by frustrating conditions of life. The main function of this mechanism is therefore to supply the individual or the group with a basis of security. This is the meaning of the group's or individual's reversion to an old pattern of behaviour. In other words, the present situation, superseding by its complexity the limit of the group's adaptability, requires the reversion to an earlier simpler form of adjustment.

Erich Fromm's thesis on Nazism may be given as an illustrative example of how the concept of regression has been applied to this phenomenon. The perspective of individual freedom opened up by the Renaissance and the Reformation has, according to Fromm, reached a critical point in our era. The thirst for freedom arose in modern man as a reaction from medieval society; it grew up in step with the dissolution of the primary bonds characteristic of the medieval community, and in step with the weakening of the integrating forces of religion. But, as Fromm notices, if some results of this wide process led to modern democracy, some others led to social disintegration. Modern society has not supplied the individual with integrating values strong enough to compensate for the loss of the bonds of the medieval community. Thus, in many contemporary societies, the need for freedom has gradually become aimless. The individual is free to realize himself, feeling, at the same time, that there is nothing outside to give sense to his life, and thus to separate his freedom from vacuum and nothingness. Here Fromm rightly points out that as long as freedom meant freedom *from* (medieval anti-individualistic society) the experience of freedom in modern man had a full meaning. The moment of crisis is marked by the projection of the experience of freedom into the future, as freedom *for*. To this type of freedom modern society has failed to give a satisfactory answer. The main symptom of this crisis is shown in the insecurity, loneliness and fear of personal responsibility unavoidably implied in the experience of freedom in contemporary society in which the socially and spiritually integrative values are on the verge of disappearance.

The direction in which the crisis of freedom is solved, suggests the Dostoevskian formula outlined in *The Grand Inquisitor* (Brothers Karamazov), escape from freedom into security by an indiscriminate acceptance of external authority.

Nazism is, according to Fromm, one of the historical forms of this escape from freedom. The individual escapes the burdens of freedom and responsibility by his unconditional surrender to a despot and by his uncritical acceptance of a body of secular beliefs and myths arranged for him by an authoritarian régime. In this case, regression consists in the fact that the urgent need for integration and belongingness provokes a reversion of some groups to a pre-rationalist and pre-individualist type of civilization.

There is no doubt that Nazism is partly determined by the fear of freedom and responsibility in contemporary man and by its positive aspect as an escape into authoritarianism. Fromm's only

mistake is that he lays too great a stress on the importance of this process in the psycho-genesis of Nazism. Consequently he completely fails to see an opposite process which has been taking place in modern society parallel to that described by him as 'fear of freedom.' This is the type of integration produced by modern society which is—as E. Durkheim suggests—a counterbalancing process to the disintegration and specialization inherent in large-scale organizations. We can talk therefore about excessive integration, and responsibility existing in contemporary man side by side with excessive freedom and lack of responsibility. Paradoxically enough, this process has also contributed to the rise of Nazism. This has happened in two main ways: On the psychological level it has gradually led to the annihilation of the individual's personality by the weakening of his critical mind. On the social plane it has gradually created a type of civilization whose main characteristics consist in a high degree of inter-individual dependence—a factory type of society. This made it all the easier for the Nazi leaders to create a highly integrated society. . . .

Fromm considers the concept of authoritarian character as the key concept in the psychology of Nazism. Generally speaking, the authoritarian character is the outcome of the structuration of a series of mental factors produced mainly by the process of regression. Anxiety, insecurity, and repressed desire for belongingness, are a few of them. The main point is that the structuring of these factors forms the basis for an individual as well as for a social authoritarian character. The latter is defined for the first time by Fromm as a structural characteristic of a group.

The main trait of an authoritarian

character consists in an ambivalent attitude towards authority. This means that the authoritarian personality and group fall into the extremes of dominance and submissiveness. On the political plane, an ambivalent attitude towards authority leads to an authoritarian organization. For in this type of organization, based on a rigid hierarchy of power, the individual can satisfy both his need for belongingness-submissiveness by his complete integration with the group and by his obedience towards the higher-ups, and, at the same time, his need for dominance towards those below him in the system.

With regard to the social basis of the authoritarian character, Fromm concentrates his attention on the lower-middle classes which, according to him, form the background of Nazism. . . . We look at this problem from a different angle. Nazism is the outcome of the German group as a whole. It is the whole group that undergoes a process of regression. Therefore the group as such is liable to authoritarian behaviour.

One can, however, distinguish various levels of crystallization of the authoritarian character. The post-war German group as a whole constitutes the first level. In this case the authoritarian traits form a loose structure; they are, so to speak, in a floating state. The German lower-middle classes represent a new level in the structuration of various authoritarian traits. At this level, the structuration takes on a more permanent character than in the German group as a whole. The reasons for this are various. One can say in general that these classes suffered more than others from the effects of the economic crisis, and therefore they were to a greater extent affected by the process of regression. There is, however, one class which felt the effects of the economic crisis even more than the lower-middle classes—the working class. And in spite of this, one can say that the working class suffered less from the feeling of insecurity than other classes. For, unlike any other class, this class had a social philosophy on which it hung its desires for security. The German working class, like any other European working class, had long before the outcome of Nazism built up another type of authoritarian character which forms the basis of Communism.

The third level in the structuration of the authoritarian factors is formed by the *déclassé* group of post-war Germany. One finds in these people additional reasons for insecurity and need for belongingness. Finally, the highest concentration of authoritarian traits is realized in a series of abnormal personalities such as Hitler, Hess, Goebbels, who had displayed throughout their lives pathological forms of authoritarian behaviour. Thus the authoritarian character emerges in four stages of intensity and purity. It is seen firstly in a diluted form in the German group as a whole, then reaches higher and higher degrees of intensity in the lower-middle classes, in the sociopathic group (*déclassés*), and finally in the psychopathic group. Nazism arises as the integration of these superimposed levels of authoritarian behaviour within German society.

In this essay ALAN BULLOCK of Oxford sets
forth the theory of National Socialism. Hitler,
Bullock asserts, was a man of deep conviction who
was sincerely committed to a few basic ideas upon
which he constructed his Third Reich. Is the argument
that Hitler was driven by convictions necessarily
at variance with the view that he was an opportunist?
What are the implications of Hitler's ideas for
Nazi practices at home and abroad?*

The Theory of Nazism:
Hitler's Basic Ideas

To spend time discussing Hitler's political ideas at first sight appears per-
verse. The character of Hitler's leadership, with its emphasis upon irrational
and emotional motives in politics, and
the character of the Nazi movement,
with its insistence upon force and its
contempt for ideas, both suggest that it
is to Nazi tactics and technique that one
should turn for an explanation of their
success in securing and maintaining
power. Moreover, the unoriginality of
Hitler's ideas, borrowed from earlier
writers (frequently unconsciously and
always without acknowledgement) or
simply picked up from the current shib-
boleths of radical and anti-Semitic talk
in Central Europe, has led most students
of Nazism either to dismiss them as not
worth serious attention or to spend their
time in tracing the sources from which
they were taken.

There is much force in these arguments. But it is worth recalling that
Hitler himself always laid great stress
upon what he called the *weltanschaulich*
element in Nazism. 'The victory of a
party is a change of government. The
victory of a *Weltanschauung* is a revolution.' It was in terms of the second that
Hitler always described the Nazis' coming to power in 1933, and throughout
his speeches it is to this National-Socialist *Weltanschauung* that he persistently
refers as the essential characteristic both
of the Nazi Party and the Nazi revolu-

* From "The Political Ideas of Adolf Hitler" by Alan Bullock in Maurice Baumont, John
H. E. Fried, and Edmond Vermeil (eds.), *The Third Reich*, published under the auspices of the
International Council for Philosophy and Humanistic Studies and with the assistance of UNESCO
(New York, 1955), pp. 350–356, 358–359, 362–363, 367–369, 376–378.

tion. If it is objected that this Nazi *Weltanschauung* was in fact no more than propaganda, it is fair to reply that, even if this is true, it was propaganda of a distinctive type, and that its success in Germany was such as to place Hitler among the greatest masters of political propaganda in history. In analysing his success as a propagandist it is a mistake to concentrate all our attention on the techniques he employed and to ignore the specific content of the appeal which drew more than a third of the German people to vote for Hitler in a free and contested election. Even as propaganda, Hitler's ideas would be well worth examination, if only because of the uncanny success they enjoyed.

In fact, however, there is no reason to suppose that Hitler was insincere in the ideas to which he gave expression in *Mein Kampf* and his many speeches. Hitler was, after all, an intellectual, in the double sense that he lived intensely in the world of his own thoughts and that words and ideas were the instruments of his power. In striking contrast to the remarkable opportunism of his political tactics and the variability of his political programme, he showed considerable consistency in adhering to certain ideas and conceptions throughout twenty-five years of political activity. In *Mein Kampf* Hitler wrote: 'When a man has reached his thirtieth year he has still a great deal to learn. That is obvious. But henceforward what he learns will principally be an amplification of his basic ideas.' Broadly speaking, this is true of Hitler himself, and it is with the discovery of these basic ideas that this article is concerned. . . .

The basis of Hitler's political beliefs was a crude Darwinism.

'Man has become great through struggle. The first fundamental of any rational *Weltanschauung* is the fact that on earth and in the universe force alone is decisive. Whatever goal man has reached is due to his originality plus his brutality. . . . There will never be a solution of the German problem until we return to the three fundamental principles which control the existence of every nation: The concept of struggle, the purity of blood, and the ingenuity of the individual.'

These three principles provide a key not only to Hitler's own beliefs, but also to what he most disliked in other people's views.

'Unfortunately, the contemporary world stresses internationalism instead of the innate values of race, democracy, and the majority instead of the worth of the great leader. Instead of everlasting struggle the world preaches cowardly pacifism and everlasting peace. These three things are the causes of the downfall of all humanity.'

The easiest way to approach Hitler's political ideas is by the closer examination of each of these three antitheses— struggle *v.* pacifism; race *v.* internationalism; inequality and individuality *v.* democracy. . . .

Struggle is not only the sole condition upon which man preserves his life, it is also the basis of all his achievement. 'Only through struggle has man raised himself *above* the animal world.' Or in the words of *Mein Kampf:* 'Man must realise that a fundamental law of necessity reigns throughout the whole realm of Nature, and that his existence is subject to the law of eternal struggle and strife.' For all man's noblest virtues, the heroic virtues—loyalty, self-sacrifice, endurance, faith—and his greatest achievements in art, the sciences, politics, and economics arise from and are nourished by this unremitting competition. Without this goad, without the difficulties which he is forced to overcome in order to survive, man would sink back to the level of the herd and achieve nothing. 'Man has become great through perpetual struggle.' The corollary is valid too. Humanitarianism, pacifism, non-resistance to evil, the Christian virtues of love and humility are so many disguises for weakness, cowardice, and irresolution. 'In perpetual peace man's greatness must decline.'

It follows from this, obviously, that 'through all the centuries force and power are the determining factors. . . . Only force rules. Force is the first law.' Force, however, is more than the decisive fact in any situation; it is force which also creates right. 'Always before God and the world, the stronger has the right to carry through what he wills. History proves: He who has not the strength—him the "right in itself" profits not a whit.' The practical application of such a view is not difficult to see. . . .

The insistence upon race, perhaps the most characteristic feature of the Nazi *Weltanschauung*, represents one of Hitler's most deep-seated beliefs. Race, as Hitler uses the word, has little to do with biological science, although he frequently claims scientific authority for what he says. Its real role is that of a myth, as Hitler later admitted in a conversation with Hermann Rauschning which is quoted below. And it is by its power to induce men to act as if it were true, not by the canons of historical criticism, that one should judge Hitler's description of the Aryans in *Mein Kampf.*

'Every manifestation of human culture, every product of art, science and technical skill, which we see before our eyes today, is almost exclusively the product of the Aryan creative power. This very fact fully justifies the conclusion that it was the Aryan alone who founded a superior type of humanity; therefore he represents the archetype of what we understand by the term, MAN. He is the Prometheus of mankind, from whose shining brow the divine spark of genius has at all times flashed forth. . . .'

According to Hitler's version of history, the Aryans subjugated inferior races (Who, When, Where are questions brushed aside) and treated them virtually as slaves.

'While he ruthlessly maintained his position as their master, the Aryan not only remained master but he also maintained and advanced civilisation. For this depended exclusively on his inborn abilities, and therefore, on his preservation of the Aryan race as such. . . . For it is never by war that nations are ruined, but by the loss of their powers of resistance, which are exclusively a characteristic of pure racial blood. In this world everything that is not of sound racial stock is like chaff.' . . .

Thus Hitler's views on race are used to justify both the right of the German people to ride rough-shod over such inferior peoples as the uncouth Slavs and the degenerate French, and the right of the Nazis, representing an *élite* sifted and tested by the struggle for power, to rule over the German people. This explains how it is that Hitler can refer to the Nazi seizure of power in Germany as a *racial* revolution, because it represents the replacement of one ruling caste by another. . . .

Inside Germany the idea of a racial *élite* played a considerable role in Hitler's view of the function of the Party and the SS. What amounted to a straightforward claim to unlimited power in the state was wrapped up in the myth of a pure race. Hitler characteristically delighted to give it a Wagnerian colouring. What he wanted to do, so he told Rauschning, was to found an Order, and this he claimed was the true interpretation of Wagner's 'Parsifal,' in which the Order of the Knights protected the

Holy Grail of pure blood and the King, Amfortas, was suffering from the incurable ailment of corrupted blood.

The essential relationship which Hitler expressed in his use of the word 'race' was inequality. . . .

The fact that democracy and such international institutions as the League of Nations were founded upon the denial of this view and the assertion of equality between men and nations were sufficient to condemn them in Hitler's eyes. . . .

In an interview with the *New York Times,* Hitler summed up his view [of the racial community] in the phrase: 'The underlying idea is to do away with egoism and to lead people into the sacred collective egoism which is the nation' [the *Volk*][1]. . . .

It is this mystical sense of community which unites the Party and binds it to the people.

'To others it seems a riddle, a mystery— this force that ever unites these hundreds of thousands, that gives them the strength to endure distress, pain, and privation. They can conceive of this only as the result of an order issued by the state. They are wrong! It is not the state which has created us; we fashioned for ourselves our state. For to one we may appear to be a party; to another an organisation; to a third something else, but in truth we are the German people. . . . So, on this evening let us pledge ourselves at every hour, on every day, only to think of Germany, of *Volk* and *Reich,* of our great nation. Our German *Volk, Sieg-Heil!*'

Finally, this setting up, not of the state, but of the *Volk* as a moral absolute overrides all other values.

[1] The German word *Volk* is usually translated as nation or people, and has been so translated here, but these English equivalents do not convey the suggestion of the primitive, instinctive tribal community of blood and soil—by comparison with such modern and artificial constructions as the state—in which Hitler's use of the word carries with it in the German.

The same criterion was applied to justice as to truth.

'The task of the Government is the maintenance of the people, the protection of the race and care for the race; all its other tasks are conditioned by this primary duty. It is only within the framework of this fixed *Weltanschauung* that justice can be, or can be allowed to be, independent. . . .

As Frick, the Minister of the Interior, summed up: '*Recht* is what benefits the German people, *Unrecht*[2] is that which harms it.' Or, to quote two of Hitler's remarks to Rauschning: 'Justice is a means of ruling. Conscience is a Jewish invention. It is a blemish, like circumcision.' . . .

The metaphor which dominates all Hitler's political thought is that of an army. He sees the state always as an instrument of power. Whatever conduces to discipline, unity, strength, action is good; whatever threatens to weaken these attributes is evil. It is to the Army, therefore, that he looks for the pattern of political organisation, and here that he finds the origin of the *Führerprinzip* —the leadership principle—upon which the National-Socialist state was to be built up. . . .

Once the Nazis came to power, the *Führerprinzip,* originally worked out in the organisation of the Party, was applied, not without much confusion, to the political leadership of the nation. From the state of weakness and dissension which was characteristic of democratic Germany 'we have to learn our lesson: one will must dominate us, we must form a single unity; our discipline must weld us together; one obedience, one subordination must fill us all, for above us stands the nation.' 'Our constitution,' wrote Nazi Germany's leading

[2] The two German words mean "right" and "wrong."—*Ed.*

lawyer, 'is the will of the *Führer*.' No rational justification of this is provided either by Hitler himself or by other Nazi writers. It is simply stated in the baldest terms that the *Führer* is the incarnation of the unity of the *Volk*, and that he is 'responsible' solely to the German people, without any suggestion of how this assertion is to be tested or the responsibility enforced. As Professor Baynes says in his edition of Hitler's *Speeches:*

'The essential link which in the National-Socialist theory of the state unites the people with the *Führer* is a mystical conception. The people on a basis of common blood creates a community and as such possesses a spirit—a *Volksgeist*—which is rooted in national history and national character. That spirit of the people may indeed be falsified and misled; it remains however anchored in the subconsciousness of the people until the time when a Leader arises who is profoundly inspired by a realisation of the uncorrupted *Volksgeist* which he can then evoke once more from the people's subconsciousness; by this power of evocation he demonstrates his autonomous immediate title to Leadership. . . . He is no representative to whom the people has given a mandate; he is the incarnation of the Spirit of the People, and it is only through his interpretation that the People is led to a full realisation of itself.'

This is a faithful summary not of Nazi propaganda, but of sober constitutional and legal opinion as it was expressed in the standard text-books of the Third Reich. That it was not just a piece of sublime mysticism and nonsense (as Castlereagh described the Holy Alliance) is demonstrated by the sort of claim Hitler was able to make as early as July 1934, when, after the purge of Roehm and the other SA leaders, he declared:

'If anybody reproaches me and asks why I did not resort to the regular courts of justice for conviction of the offenders, then all that I can say to him is this: in this hour I was responsible for the fate of the German people, and thereby I became the Supreme Justiciar (*oberster Gerichtsherr*) of the German people.'

Hitler's justification of his own autocratic power is always phrased in terms of this same mystical sense of mission, yet he is always careful to claim that it is rooted in the people. Speaking to the *Reichstag* at the end of his first year of office, Hitler told them:

'Since that historic hour, I have never for a moment regarded the task that became mine otherwise than as a commission entrusted to me by the whole of the German people, even if millions, whether consciously or unconsciously, were not then clear about this fact or if they did not wish to accept it as the truth.' . . .

For Hitler, the Jew was a mythical figure, evil incarnate, the figure into which he projected all that he hated and feared. Like all obsessions, it was not a partial but a total explanation. The Jew is everywhere, he is responsible for everything. An interesting example of this is to be found in an early speech of 1922.

'The master stroke of the Jew was to claim the leadership of the fourth estate; he founded the Movement both of the Social Democrats and of the Communists. His policy was two-fold and he had his apostles in both camps. Amongst the parties of the Right he encouraged those features which were most repugnant to the people—the passion for money, unscrupulous methods in trade which were employed so ruthlessly as to give rise to the proverb: "Business, too, marches over corpses." And the Jew attacked the parties of the Right through the blood of their members. It was from the Jews that the upper classes took their wives. The result was that in a short time it was precisely the ruling class which became in its attitude completely estranged from its own people.

'And this fact gave the Jew his opportunity with the parties of the Left. Here he played the part of the common demagogue. . . . And one can see constantly how wonderfully the stock exchange Jew and the leader of the workers cooperate. They both pursue one common policy and one single aim. Moses Kohn on the one side encourages his association to resist the workers' demands, while his brother Isaac in the factory incites the masses. . . . The stock exchange organ seeks without intermission to encourage fevered speculation and unparalleled "corners" in grain and the people's food, while the workman's newspaper lets off all its guns on the masses, telling them that bread is dearer and this, that and the other is dearer: Up Proletarians, endure it no longer!

'This process means the utter destruction not only of economic life, but of the people. . . . The backbone of its independence, its own national economic life is to be destroyed, that it may the more surely relapse into the golden fetters of the interest slavery of the Jewish race.'

Hitler's anti-Semitism is the master-idea which embraces the whole span of his thought. In whatever direction one follows Hitler's train of thought, sooner or later one encounters the satanic figure of the Jew. Democracy is Jewish—the secret domination of the Jew. Bolshevism and Social-Democracy, capitalism and the 'interest-slavery' of the money-lender; parliamentarianism and the freedom of the press; liberalism and internationalism; anti-militarism and the class war; modernism in art ('Kultur-Bolschevismus'), prostitution and miscegenation—all are instruments devised by the Jew to subdue the Aryan peoples to his rule. One of Hitler's favourite phrases, which he claimed to have taken from Mommsen, was: 'The Jew is the ferment of decomposition in peoples.' This points to the fundamental fact

about the Jew in Hitler's eyes: unlike the Aryan, the Jew is incapable of founding a state, and so incapable of anything creative. He can only imitate and steal —or destroy in the spirit of envy.

'The Jew has never founded any civilisation, though he has destroyed hundreds. He possesses nothing of his own creation to which he can point. Everything he has is stolen. Foreign peoples, foreign workmen build him his temples; it is foreigners who shed their blood for him. He has no art of his own; bit by bit he has stolen it all from other peoples. He does not even know how to preserve the precious things others have created. . . . In the last resort it was the Aryan alone who could form states and set them on their path to future greatness. All this the Jew cannot do. And because he cannot do it, therefore all his revolutions must be international. They must spread as a pestilence spreads. Already he has destroyed Russia; now it is the turn of Germany and with his envious instinct for destruction he seeks to disintegrate the national spirit of the Germans and to pollute their blood.'

One could pursue this theme for a long time and illustrate it with a thousand quotations. But here clearly one passes out of the realm of rational ideas into that of the mythological and the fantastic, never far below the surface in Hitler's thought. So we come back to the same point from which we began—race and blood, struggle and domination, the Aryan v. the Jew, the *Herrenmenschen* v. the *Untermenschen*.[3] It is a crude and ugly picture of the world, but it is one which—as the history of the past quarter-century shows—has more attraction than we like to admit, 'so much less,' as Mill pointed out, 'do the majority of mankind prefer liberty than power.'

3 "Supermen" v. "Lowermen."—*Ed.*

The book from which this selection is taken is required reading for thousands of German students. It is assigned because of all the books on the subject it gives the clearest and most candid picture of what life was actually like under Hitler. HANNAH VOGT (1900–   ), the author of several studies on German politics and law, was educated at the universities of Göttingen, Hamburg, and Marburg. Since 1954 she has been a director of the Office of Political Education in the state of Hessen. What is the connection between this description of Nazi practices and Bullock's account of Hitler's theories? *

Life in the Third Reich

Young people in Germany often receive contradictory information about the true conditions of life in the Third *Reich*. History books, documents, films, and magazines describe it as ugly and horrible, and make it hard to believe that such a thing once happened in their fatherland. Their elders, on the other hand, often tell them that most people lived well in the Third *Reich*, that people had jobs and earned good money, and that those were the best years within memory, at least up to the war. Nothing much could be felt of the terror.

Puzzled by these reports, young people may well ask that these contradictions be resolved.

When Hitler seized power, the world

depression had in fact already passed its peak. Conditions everywhere had begun to improve more or less quickly. Nevertheless, unemployment did not disappear by itself, and generally government intervention provided the means of revitalizing the economy without endangering the currency of the country.

In Germany, the construction of the *Reichsautobahn* (superhighway) was begun as one of these government ventures. The first relevant decree had been enacted by June 1933, but publicity for building such highways had begun as early as 1924. In 1926, an association founded exclusively for this purpose advanced a proposal for an autobahn from Hamburg to Basle. By 1932, a super-

* From *The Burden of Guilt: A Short History of Germany, 1914–1945* by Hannah Vogt, translated by Herbert Strauss. Copyright © 1964 by Oxford University Press, Inc. Reprinted by permission. Pp. 147–150, 154, 157–163, 168–175, 212, 220–223, 225–234.

highway linking Cologne with Bonn was opened for traffic, although without the great, nation-wide fanfare which became the custom later on. Hitler took up existing plans, but, for military reasons, placed his main emphasis on building an east-west connection. An outstanding civil engineering expert, Dr. Todt, built the autobahns and achieved great technological success. No doubt, Hitler also hoped to build himself a monument for future generations in the *Reichsautobahn*. And, indeed, even today there are people in Germany who remember Hitler primarily as the "builder of the *Reichsautobahn*," and refuse to believe that he murdered millions of innocent people, started a world conflagration, and rent Germany in two. . . .

From the start, re-armament played a great role in creating new jobs. Before Hitler even assumed power, Germany had been granted parity in armaments. Hitler followed it up by re-introducing universal conscription in 1935.

A few months later, the Compulsory Labor Service Law was enacted, which obligated each young German, in the public interest, to serve for six months in the Labor Service. For this purpose, an organization called the *Reich* Labor Service (*Reichsarbeitsdienst* or RAD) was established. Compulsory labor service also extended to women, drew a considerable number of unemployed workers off the labor market, and thus provided cheap labor for jobs which did not attract a sufficient number of free workers. Women, for example, were directed mainly to do housework in peasant homes. It also served as pre-military training for young men. The Labor Service embodied Hitler's ideal of subjecting men to total service and of thoroughly militarizing all areas of life. This latter aspect of the Labor Service affected

men more than women, for the latter often found it a truly enriching experience to spend six months with women of the same age from all walks of life and all occupations.

In September 1936, Hitler was able to announce to the *Reich* Party Congress that unemployment had been reduced from six million to one million. This made a lasting impression on the population at large. Anybody who had been out of work and starving for years could easily believe that another "golden age" had arrived, for he now held a regular job and received secure pay. Such personal reminiscences tend to make people ignore the fact that the economy could have recovered without a dictator (as demonstrated by other countries), or that the re-armament factor might well become a threat to peace in the future.

This trend could already be observed in the Four Year Plan which Hitler announced at the same *Reich* Party Congress. He called for German economic self-sufficiency (autarky) in a maximum number of fields: "Within four years, Germany must be made independent of foreign countries in all those raw materials which, with German efficiency, our chemical and machine tool industries as well as our mining concerns can produce by themselves."

This program of self-sufficiency led to the mass production of artifical rubber (called buna) and synthetic gasoline. Since this policy was principally dictated by military rather than economic considerations, Göring, the airforce expert, and not Schacht as Minister of Economics, was put in charge of its execution. . . .

In an analysis of life in the Third *Reich* cultural policies may appear comparatively secondary; for the population at large was more interested in securing jobs and adequate incomes than in questioning whether writers were allowed to publish, or painters to paint abstract pictures, for example. A comprehensive view of a period must, however, include its intellectual, as well as its economic, military, or technological achievements.

There was one respect, admittedly, in which cultural policies coincided directly with the interest of the nation as a whole. That was in the production of the kind of information it obtained from its newspapers. Insufficient, biased, false, or exaggerated information will create an untrue image of reality. Readers of this type of information are misled and easily manipulated by the authorities. Aided by the so-called Editors Law, Goebbels through his Ministry of Popular Enlightenment and Propaganda was in absolute control of the German press. The German people were told only what he approved of. He had perfected the technique of "regulating the language" so well even before the Second World War that he prescribed to the press, down to minute details, whether and how an item was to be presented or emphasized. Hate campaigns, political slander, or purposeful lies could thus be "produced" and spread at any time in any manner as desired.

Poets and writers fared little better than journalists. The book-burning which was organized at the Berlin Opera Square on May 10, 1933, and considered important enough for radio coverage, had sounded the keynote for the cultural policies of the Third *Reich*. Mouthing campfire slogans, students threw into the fire works of those authors who had been derisively labeled as "racially alien," including Karl Marx, Sigmund Freud, Erich Kaestner, Erich Maria Remarque, Friedrich Wilhelm Foerster, the Nobel prize winner Carl von Ossietzky, and many others. Later on in September, the control of the Propaganda Ministry was extended to all areas of cultural life through a law which created a *Reich* Culture Chamber, to be presided over by Goebbels. Artists were forced to join one of the branch chambers controlled by this Chamber (*Reich* Literature Chamber, *Reich* Music Chamber, *Reich* Radio Chamber, etc.). Exclusion from a chamber, in effect, meant the end of all professional activities. When the artist Schmidt-Rottluff was ordered to stop painting, compliance with the order was enforced by the Gestapo!

These devices served primarily to exclude the Jews from cultural life. As a result, untold numbers of poets, writers, musicians, conductors, actors, architects, and painters fled abroad. The emigration of Jewish artists not only inflicted a great loss on all areas of German culture but also disgraced Germany before the entire world. In Germany only a few voices were raised in protest against this lunatic persecution. . . .

But Hitler and Goebbels were not satisfied with driving the Jews from German cultural life. They also wanted to influence German artists and artistic tastes directly. Goebbels ordered the production of motion pictures spreading antisemitism (e.g. "The Jew Süss"). He outlawed art criticism and wanted it replaced by "meditations on art," i.e. mere descriptions of subject matter. Some journalists made a virtue of necessity: their descriptions damned more effectively than any critical review!

Hitler fancied himself an expert in the fine arts. He hated not only abstract art but all modern painting. Dubbing them "degenerate," he had hundreds of pictures removed from museums and galleries. To house the new "racially correct" art, he built the House of German Art in Munich, where he sponsored annual exhibitions of art that suited his taste; these consisted mainly of Hitler portraits, outsized canvases of Storm Troopers on the march, and Labor Service gangs carrying spades over their shoulders, idealized peasant scenes, pictures glorifying Nordic man, and sweetly sentimental nudes.

Such "art," together with political jingles by people like Anacker, the Horst Wessel biographies, the "blood-and-soil" novels, and the rest of the racially correct elaborations of Nazi culture, well deserve to remain forgotten. Race hatred and self-glorification have proved uncreative. . . .

The shameful persecution of the Jews extended equally to the sciences. Jewish university teachers (including such outstanding Nobel prize winners as James Franck, Albert Einstein, and Otto Warburg) were driven from the country. Books by Jewish authors were removed from the libraries, and references to them forbidden. Contrary to the prevailing belief of free scientists in the universal validity of the methods and results of the natural sciences, Nazi university teachers claimed that natural science, too, was determined by race. Philipp Lenard, a Nobel prize winner, wrote a *German Physics* in 1936: in spite of all this, research in the natural sciences continued to be carried out on the basis of discoveries by Jewish scholars such as Albert Einstein and Niels Bohr (who had a Jewish mother). Otto Hahn, for example, succeeded in 1938 in splitting the uranium atom, thus making a significant contribution to modern atomic science. . . .

Hitler himself had relatively little use for learning and education. Where Lenin had issued the order "Learn, learn, learn!" (it decorates the walls of all Soviet schools) and thus placed a premium on effort and ambition, Hitler summarized his ideas on education as:

My pedagogy is hard. The weak must be chiseled away. In my "Order Castles"[1] young people will grow up who will frighten the world. I want a violent, arrogant, unafraid, cruel youth, who must be able to suffer pain. Nothing weak or tender must be left in them. Their eyes must bespeak once again the free, magnificent beast of prey. I want my young people strong and beautiful. I shall train them in all kinds of athletics, for I want youth that are athletic —that is first and foremost. Thus will I erase a thousand years of human domestication. Thus will I face the pure and noble raw material. Thus I can create the new. I do not want an intellectual education. With knowledge I will spoil the young. I would vastly prefer them to learn only what they absorbed voluntarily as they followed their play instinct. They shall learn to overcome the fear of death through the most arduous tests. This is the [historic] stage of heroic youth.

. . . Hitler's real plans [for Christian Churches] were well known to his inner circle, where he dropped all pretense: "The churches may take command of the German in the hereafter. The German nation, through its Fuehrer, takes command of the German in this world!" Hitler told Rauschning that he would completely stamp out Christianity in Germany. "Whether the German people retained its Jewish faith in Christ, with His soft morality of pity, or whether it believed strongly and heroically in god in nature, god in the nation, god in destiny, god in the blood" was a question which would decide its very destiny. . . .

The Nazi struggle against the churches

1 "Order Castles" (*Ordensburgen*) were training schools for the future Nazi elite. The name was derived from the medieval castles built by such orders as the Teutonic Knights, and it played upon adolescent romanticism and perverted youth movement traditions. *Trl.*

ended with the outbreak of the Second World War. Hitler shied away from public controversies, for he feared they might impair the morale of his soldiers. Yet, he did not lose sight of his final goal and ordered plans to be drawn up which aimed at the final annihilation of both faiths. . . .

The law is one of the means by which power is checked and limited. It is therefore hardly surprising that Hitler, with his lust for power, hated and despised the law above all else. At best, he considered it a means of controlling the populace. To him, the human conscience was a Jewish invention, and he boasted in his "secret conversations" that he would not hesitate to commit perjury, or conclude and break treaties "in cold blood" many times a day. Hitler's contempt for the law contrasted sharply with his respect for the Germanic tribes: the ancient Germans held the law sacred, whether customary or statutory, and would rather have killed their kings than broken their laws.

Hitler was, of course, shrewd enough not to reveal to the masses that he "despised justice and morality." Instead, he tried to hide his misdeeds behind a screen of legal verbiage. To this end, he very cleverly adopted a technique of pseudo-legality which was well calculated to play upon the German mind. Most Germans believed that a law or command per se had to be just. It was by such pure legal formalities that "unjust laws" were accepted in Germany. Such laws were not based on the idea of justice but on the principle that "law was what was useful to the nation." Again, it was up to Hitler alone to determine how this usefulness should be applied. . . .

To interpret the law "correctly," judges were ordered to consider the Nazi *Weltanschauung*, the utterances of the Fuehrer, and the so-called "healthy sense of the people." Any arbitrary decision could be rationalized with such principles. . . .

Still more pernicious was the way in which an ever increasing number of people were tortured or executed without trial or sentence for no worse crime than unorthodox opinions or "impurity of race." This development took place before the eyes of the entire German people.

What, then, of concentration camps? When they were established, people might have believed in good faith that they were needed for the "restoration of public order and security," to quote Article 48 of the Constitution. However, when the Nazis had firm control of all effective power—the police, the armed forces, the civil service—after all political opponents had totally disappeared from public life, after elections had "proved" that 98 per cent of the people favored Hitler—why were concentration camps still kept up? Why were they even increased in number? . . .

It was not due to either negligence or accident that concentration camps continued to exist past the time when people no longer had any reason to fear the "Red danger." They formed a well-calculated part of the system. To quote Hitler:

Terrorism is an effective political tool. I shall not deprive myself of it merely because these simple-minded bourgeois "softies" take offense. These so-called atrocities render it unnecessary for me to conduct hundreds of thousands of individual raids against mutinous and dissatisfied people. People will think twice before opposing us, if they know what awaits them in the camps.

The exact fate of these unfortunate victims—the political opponents, the trade-union leaders, the clergymen, the monks, Jehovah's Witnesses, and pacifists

—was only hinted at among people in the Third *Reich*. Those who returned from these hells had to keep silent to avoid renewed danger to themselves. In all probability, their stories would not even have been believed. Yet, it was known, or could have been known, that prisoners were sent to camps without a trial and for indefinite periods, and that there was no right of appeal.

In this day, the trials before German courts of former concentration camp commandants and guards have given all of us an insight into the grisly realities of these camps. Hundreds of witnesses have revealed how limitless power unleashed evil instincts. "In the camps, everything human disappeared. We were merely objects. No normal mortal can imagine how we were treated," said one of the witnesses. Blows, beatings, and kickings were part of the daily routine, so much so that one of the accused camp-torturers declared during his trial that such measures did not constitute mistreatment! Prisoners had to do "gymnastics" until they fainted with exhaustion, or, for hours on end, had to give the Saxon salute, i.e. remain in a deep knee-bend with arms laced behind their heads. These were merely the harmless "jokes" indulged in by the camp guards. Prisoners were whipped for the slightest offense—or for none at all; they were strapped on a rack, and ordered to execute knee-bends after being whipped; no less frequently prisoners were trussed up with hands tied behind their backs.

The life of a prisoner counted for nothing. Prisoners disliked by the guards were arbitrarily selected for injections (*abgespritzt*), which means they were murdered through injections of Phenol or Evipan, only one of a number of methods of killing. Prisoners were often trampled to death with nailed boots, or drowned in cesspools, or driven into the electrically charged barbed-wire fences of the camps, or, in an especially bestial manner, hosed to death with high-pressure water hoses. Innumerable witnesses have placed all these ghastly details on court records during many months of trials, and the defendants have admitted them.

In this system human beings had turned into "things" to such an extent that the administrative S.S. bureaus concerned "calculated the profitability" of prisoners. A prisoner was expected to live on average for nine months. During this time, according to calculations, the productivity of each prisoner was calculated to yield 1,631 Marks for the Nazi state (the total includes the profit gained from the "careful utilization of the corpse").

The trials conducted against Hitler's underlings in Ulm, Bayreuth, and Bonn have induced many Germans to ask: "How was it possible? Were there so many unrecognized sadists, criminals, and murderers among us?" There is only one answer: if the state had been based on law (a *Rechtsstaat*), they would not have found the opportunities to indulge their base instincts with impunity. The Nazi state, based on injustice (an *Unrechtsstaat*), gave them these opportunities. It handed them the victims after depriving the latter of all right and protection, and it placed a premium on sadism and cruelty. It was the bullies and the murderers who advanced in this system, not the decent citizens. . . .

One of the camp guards (revealingly nicknamed "Iron Gustav") testified at his trial: "In 1939, Sachsenhausen was visited by the President of the People's Court, Freisler [then the highest jurist in the country]. We showed him everything, the rack, the whipping, everything. Upon leaving Freisler said: 'Your prisoners strike me as still rather cocky. You simply have a recreation home here.' This was a confirmation for us. Everything was O.K."

Physicians on duty in the concentration camps lost all sense of values in the atmosphere of general lawlessness. They killed thousands of innocent human beings by injecting poison, or performed senseless and painful medical experiments on helpless victims who died miserably as a result. Thus had physicians abandoned their proper profession as healers.

While all these horrors took place, only a few people knew about the full extent of the atrocities. Yet, the mere two letters KL (*Konzentrations-Lager*) —the abbreviation used by the S.S., instead of the popular KZ—inspired terror, exactly as Hitler had wanted it, as his own words bear testimony. The terror threatened anybody who dared to offer even the slightest resistance to the two main doctrines. Those ready—or at least pretending—to believe that "the Jews are our misfortune," and that "the Fuehrer can do no wrong," were able to stay out of danger.

Nothing that must be reported about the Third *Reich* is so hard to grasp as the fact that nearly six million Jews were "exterminated according to plan" during this period. This figure is so monstrous that reason refuses to accept it, for the heart cannot fathom its horror. But as we must face this truth we are pursued by the nagging question as to how these monstrous deeds could have been possible. How could innocent people be treated in this fashion? How can one understand a hatred which had such terrifying consequences? . . .

For various reasons, the situation of the Jews in Germany deteriorated after the First World War: national pride had been deeply hurt and humiliated by the war-guilt clause and other articles of the Treaty of Versailles. As nationalism spread, antisemitic propaganda followed in its wake. With the adoption of parliamentary democracy, the citizen, burdened with greater responsibilities, felt insecure and searched for easy solutions and remedies for all his difficulties. Finally, increasing attention was centered on the Jews when a large number of so-called "eastern Jews" emigrated from what were once Austrian and Russian areas in Poland.

The economic dislocation of inflation and the subsequent depression combined with nationalistic passions, monarchist dreams, and anti-democratic sentiments to form the unholy alliance which was to destroy the Weimar Republic. What role did antisemitism play in this? Did Hitler grow strong because he preached the most outspoken and vulgar type of antisemitism? Was "Death to the Jews!" the slogan which sent the majority of the German people marching under his banner?

The answer to these questions is probably "No." Surely the struggle against Versailles, against the "parliamentary talking shop," and the adoption of a vague socialism played a greater role in winning masses of voters. Still, the sobering doubt remains of why the slogan "Death to the Jews!" which screamed out from many Nazi posters, and was spread by many newspapers, did not frighten more people by its undisguised brutality. . . .

Even the minds of children were poisoned by books picturing the "hellish features" of the Jew. So-called "scientific" works flooded the market in which sick and evil minds poured out their hatred without restraint. . . .

On March 28, 1933, the Nazi party bosses organized a boycott of Jewish stores. Uniformed S.A. men daubed

Jewish stars on the shop windows of Jewish stores, and picketed them with outsized signs demanding: "Don't buy from Jews!" Jewish merchants were intimidated and suffered damages, but their customers were not so easily driven away. . . .

Hitler did not dare take the next large step until the *Reich* Party Congress in Nuremberg in 1935, when the Nuremberg Laws reduced Jews to the category of second-class citizens. Marriages and extra-marital relations between Jews and "citizens of German blood" were forbidden. Racial crime (*Rassenschande*) became a favorite theme of Streicher's hate sheet "Der Stürmer." . . .

A string of similar antisemitic decrees followed upon the assassination of Ernst vom Rath, a councillor at the German legation in Paris, by Herschel Grynszpan, a Polish Jew, on November 9, 1938. It started with the burning down of synagogues in Germany by S.A. troops, acting under orders. Altogether 267 synagogues went up in flames that night; in addition, 815 stores were destroyed, 20,000 Jews arrested, and 36 killed. In his press, Goebbels had the nerve to pass off these acts of arson which he had organized and directed in person as "a spontaneous reaction of the German people." It would, however, be truer to say that many people reacted with spontaneous indignation as the scales fell from their eyes about the true character of the Nazi regime. But they were not indignant enough to resist openly.

The cue was now provided for the party leaders to put their sick fantasies into practice. By a horrible perversion of justice, the victims, the aggrieved, the despoiled—the Jews—were ordered to "atone for their crimes" with a fine of **one billion marks. Another decree stated:**

Paragraph 1: All the damage caused by the indignation of the people about the propaganda attacks of international Jewry against Nazi Germany in Jewish business premises and dwelling units on November 8, 9, and 10, 1938, is to be repaired at once by the Jewish owner, or the Jew who did business on the premises.

Paragraph 2: The expense of the repair is to be borne by the owners of the Jewish business premises and dwelling units concerned. Insurance claims by Jews of German nationality are confiscated in favor of the *Reich*.

Other orders followed in close succession. First came the Exclusion of Jews from German Economic Life, and then Jews were forbidden to engage in business or crafts and could no longer be employed in an executive capacity. The Minister of Education ordered the removal of Jewish pupils from German schools. Many cities established a so-called "Jew ban," which meant Jews were forbidden to enter certain residential sections, or to visit movie houses, museums, and theaters. . . .

This systematic and calculated chicanery was stepped up even more after the outbreak of the war. Beginning in 1940, Jews in many places could do their shopping only at fixed hours. Later, Jews were restricted to only a few designated stores. In September 1941, the Jewish Star Decree followed, according to which Jews 6 years and over had to wear in public "a hexagonal star, the size of a palm, bordered in black, made of yellow material, bearing the inscription 'Jew' in black letters, affixed to the left side of their garments at the height of the breast." The use of the star of David, a religious symbol, as a stigma was especially vindictive. . . .

It is embarrassing to enumerate the many petty humiliations to which the law was bent. In 1942 the *Reich* Law Gazette was filled with such decrees: all Jewish dwellings were to be marked by the star of David; Jews were not permitted to keep pets; Jews were forbidden to have their hair cut by Aryan barbers; Jews were not allowed to own electric appliances, record players, typewriters, bicycles; Jews were not allowed to visit heated public shelters, etc.

But these systematic, calculated annoyances had long since been overshadowed by an incomparably more terrifying threat. . . .

Beginning as early as the spring of 1940, the S.S. had re-established ghettoes in such Polish cities as Lublin, Lodz, Cracow, and Warsaw. The Jews were herded into designated parts of the towns, and the entire area was surrounded with fences and cordoned off with signs which warned: "No trespassing, Jewish quarter." At that time, Poland had 2.9 million Jews. These unfortunate people had been unable to emigrate, for they were mostly small farmers, tradesmen, and craftsmen and could not possibly obtain the money for the voyage. They fell prey as helpless victims to the S.S.

On the pattern of these Polish ghettoes, an entire ghetto-city was established in 1941 in Terezin (Theresienstadt in Bohemia). It was to serve as a forced residence for German Jews, primarily for leading Jewish functionaries. . . . This camp, like all other camps, was a well-organized hell where man's mind withered under the narrow compulsions of collective life before his body died of hunger. For many, however, Theresienstadt was only a station on the way to the extermination camps established for the "final solution of the Jewish question."

On July 31, 1941, Göring issued instructions to Heydrich, the S.D. chief, to submit a comprehensive draft for the carrying out of the "final solution of the Jewish question." . . . Among the S.S., plans were circulated for the deportation of all Jews to the island of Madagascar, off the African coast.

Since such plans were impractical, the doctrinaires around Himmler decided to "exterminate" the Jews. The minutes of a meeting held at the Grosse Wannsee to plan the "final solution" (known as the Wannsee Protocol) read as follows:

. . . The Jews should in the course of the Final Solution be taken in a suitable manner to the east for use as labor. In big labor gangs, separated by sex, the Jews capable of work will be brought to these areas for road building, in which task undoubtedly a large number will fall through natural diminution. The remnant that is finally able to survive all this—since this is undoubtedly the part with the strongest resistance—must be treated accordingly, since these people, representing a natural selection, are to be regarded as the germ cell of a new Jewish development, in case they should succeed and go free (as history has proved). In the course of the execution of the Final Solution, Europe will be combed from west to east.

Nowhere is the bureaucratic make-believe language of the S.S., the language of inhumanity, revealed more horribly than in this document. Following this blueprint, the S.S. began to call its subsequent mass murder "special treatment." Faced with tremendous numbers of absolutely helpless human beings, the executioners of the Third *Reich* were seized with a frenzy of extermination.

At first, "special treatment" consisted in mass shootings. The Jews were dragged out of their ghettoes and ordered to dig ditches in remote places. Next, every man, woman, child, and aged person had to strip naked, and carefully place his clothing and his shoes on piles. Then, five to ten people at a time had to step up together to the edge of the ditch, and were mowed down with a tommy gun. After the mass graves had filled with 500 to 1000 bodies, they were covered with lime and earth. It is reported that Himmler was so nauseated when he witnessed this "method," that he recommended from then on, as a "more humane means," the use of poison gas (to be released in vans or specially constructed chambers camouflaged as shower rooms). Suitable facilities for this form of mass extermination were constructed in the large extermination camps of Auschwitz, Maidanek, and Treblinka. Huge crematoria were built, and the bodies were burned around the clock.

To top this absolutely infernal system the Jews themselves were ordered to operate the entire machinery of murder. They had to remove the piled-up bodies from the gas chambers and to operate the crematoria. The only hope remaining to these workers in their ghastly work was, perhaps, to escape death.

Today, some people refuse to face up to these appalling facts. But can we be so cowardly as to evade even in our imaginations the suffering that real people, people such as you and I, had to bear in harsh reality?

When those Jews who were still free learned about the ultimate destinations of their deported co-religionists, they sought, by any available means, to go underground and live "illegally." . . .

For the many who found this escape barred, the end was always the same: first, work to exhaustion in factories "essential for the war," each day filled with fear that relatives incapable of work had received orders for deportation to the east. . . . This would come for everyone some day. . . . In the last moment, many chose to die by their own hands. . . . At collection points, the deportees were robbed of their last belongings. Then, for days, the trip in overcrowded cattle-cars. If Theresienstadt was the destination, it could mean a small respite. If it was one of the notorious extermination camps, incoming transports were led to "selection." Men were separated from women, children torn away from parents. The sick, the aged, the weak, and the children were sent to the left at "selection": their destiny was death. Those still considered capable of work were sent into the barracks and had to work as slaves for their miserable food until they died of hunger or epidemics, or were themselves selected for extermination. The threat of death hung ever present over all; the smell of the crematoria lay like a cloud over the camps. . . .

The S.S. guards held daily roll-calls in these camps, too, and forced the emaciated prisoners, in their garb of rags, to stand in rain, snow, sun, or wind until all inmates had been counted. Woe to any of these human beings who lost his precarious hold on life and died unnoticed in a barrack on a heap of rags! Then the prisoners were counted and re-counted and 24, even 48, hours might pass before the prisoners were allowed to disband. Those who fell down were kicked or beaten.

This lust for extermination was revealed to its full extent in the copious records where all murders were listed with bureaucratic pedantry. An S.S. Economic and Administrative Main Office was founded exclusively for such purposes as collecting and packaging all the possessions of the murdered, from tons of clothing to eye glasses, artificial teeth, gold teeth, and women's hair, and "utilizing" them. Man was not only exterminated as if he were vermin, he was also made into matter and exploited as a "source of raw material" for the war economy.

This was the result of the Final Solution:

Country	Jewish Population, September 1939	Jewish Losses	Percentage of Jewish Losses
1. Poland	3,300,000	2,800,000	85.0
2. USSR,, occupied territory	2,100,000	1,500,000	71.4
3. Rumania	850,000	425,000	50.0
4. Hungary	404,000	200,000	49.5
5. Czechoslovakia	315,000	260,000	82.5
6. France	300,000	90,000	30.0
7. Germany	210,000	170,000	81.0
8. Lithuania	150,000	135,000	90.0
9. Netherlands	150,000	90,000	60.0
10. Latvia	95,000	85,000	89.5
11. Belgium	90,000	40,000	44.4
12. Greece	75,000	60,000	80.0
13. Yugoslavia	75,000	55,000	73.3
14. Austria	60,000	40,000	66.6
15. Italy	57,000	15,000	26.3
16. Bulgaria	50,000	7,000	14.0
17. Others	20,000	6,000	30.0
	8,301,000	5,978,000	72.0

Nobody will ever fully appreciate the suffering behind these figures: the humiliations, the shame, the agony. We cannot escape it by saying that we did not know about it and had never wanted it to happen. However true this may be, where were we when we should have opposed the beginnings? One of the most impressive short stories of Leo Tolstoy bears the title: "If you let the flame rise, you will never extinguish it!" We let the flame of hatred rise and did not extinguish it while there was still time. We allowed posters and songs to spread hatred and abuse while we were still at liberty to fight against them. This first sin of omission gave rise to all the later crimes.

To the injustice committed in our name we must not add the injustice of forgetting. While relatives still mourn their dead, can we forget because the shadows of the past are painful to us? There is no restitution for such enormous suffering. But by preserving the memory of the victims, we can perform a sacred duty imposed upon us by the guilt we bear toward our Jewish fellow-citizens.

Aristotle once observed that the best way to gain insight into the nature of a government is to examine the educational system it designs for its children. The most authoritative, brief description of Nazi schools and youth movements is given by WILLIAM EBENSTEIN (1910–   ), who is now professor of politics at the University of California, Santa Barbara. He has written important books on political theory as well as incisive studies of Fascist Italy and Nazi Germany. What does this description of education and indoctrination under Hitler reveal about the ideals, plans, and purposes of the Third Reich? Is there any connection between Nazi education and Nazi foreign policy? *

Education Under Hitler

According to an editorial of the official journal of the German educators, *"Mein Kampf,* the immortal work of the Leader, is our infallible pedagogical guiding star."* In a series of police measures all German schools, from grade schools to universities, have been put under the domination of the Nazi party. . . .

The type of race science which is officially recommended by the Ministry for school libraries may be gathered from *The Poisonous Mushroom (Der Gift-pilz),* published in 1938 in Nuremberg. The poisonous mushroom is the Jew. In a series of little stories and poems the children are taught the character of the Jew. A mother teaches her child in the

beginning that "just as a single mushroom can kill a whole family, so a solitary Jew can destroy a whole village, a whole city, even an entire nation." The Jew is "the Devil in human form." One child exclaims as follows on the baptism of Jews: "I do not understand why these priests go on baptizing Jews even today. By doing so they admit a criminal mob into the churches." Another little story shows how the Jew entices little children to his home by giving them candies, but is caught by the policeman and hauled off to prison before he can abuse them. Another tale deals with a girl who is sick. Her mother sends her to a Jewish doctor. The girl first refuses because she has been told about Jewish doctors in the Hitler Youth. However, she obeys her mother. "She went to the Jewish Doctor Bernstein. Inge sits in the waiting room." She thinks of what she has been told about the Jews. "Suddenly, a girl's voice comes from the doctor's office: 'Doctor, doctor, leave me alone!' Then she hears the mocking laughter of a man. Suddenly everything is quite still. Inge has listened breathless." The doctor at last enters the waiting room. Inge screams. The face of the doctor "is the face of the Devil. There is a grin which says: 'At last I have you, little German girl!' And then the Jew goes to her. His fleshy fingers lay hold of her." But Inge, the little German girl, manages to escape and runs home. The following provides a little poetic expression of race science.

A devil goes through the land.
The Jew he is, known to us all,
As murderer of the peoples and
    polluter of the races
The terror of children in every country!

. . . Arithmetic is taught in the following manner: The Nordic blood proportion of the German people is four fifths. One third of this group is blond. How many blonds are there in the total population of sixty-six million? Or a small machine gun mows down an enemy reconnaisance unit. Of a total of two hundred and fifty shots, twenty hits are registered. Express this figure in percentages. . . .

Under a new program the magazine for grade school children, *Hilf Mit!,* is filled with even more military propaganda than it contained before. The circulation is given as five million, but officials of the organization of grade school teachers estimate that at least twelve million people read the paper, for many parents are regular readers. Therefore this paper also has the func-

tion of imbuing the parents of the children with war enthusiasm.

Essay competitions have been organized on the following topics: What Children Can Do to Help in Air-Raid and Fire Protection; How Can Children Help the War by Collecting Old Clothes, or Scrap; How Children Can Help the Farmer by Working on the Land.

The next point of attack of the new education program is the publication of pamphlets aimed to cultivate militaristic attitudes *(wehrgeistige Erziehung)*. These pamphlets have been published by the organization of grade school teachers in conjunction with the military authorities. They are so cheap (only three or four cents apiece) that individual children are encouraged to buy them. Five main topics are dealt with by these educational pamphlets: The armed forces of Greater Germany; How the army of the Leader created Greater Germany; Our Westwall is unconquerable; Volunteering for the German army; He who wants victory must be able to fight. . . .

The next point of the program states generally that the whole instructional program has to be co-ordinated with the war objectives. In the teaching of history a program has been recommended along the following lines: In the first month of the year there are two main history topics: The Leader created Great Germany; Great Germany struggling for its existence. The second month is to take up this historical topic: The Leader tore apart the chains imposed upon the German people by the enemies at Versailles. The third month of history teaching covers this topic: In the World War the enemies sought to annihilate the German people and the German Reich. And so it goes on until the climax of history teaching is reached in the eighth and last month in the fol-

lowing topic: One people—one Reich—
one Leader. The last subtopic of the
last topic is a historical appreciation of
the Leader as a military genius. . . .

In the teaching of German the essays
are written to celebrate the heroic element in war. Girls have to write on
topics concerned with what the women
can do for the folk community in time
of war.

Physics and chemistry are focused on
practical problems which will better explain to the children their tasks in air-
raid protection or fire-protection. Special
emphasis in physics and chemistry is
also given to ersatz materials, especially
those which are essential for the winning of the war. . . .

The Hitler Youth

The Nazification of German youth is
accomplished not only by the transformation of the existing educational institutions and the development of new
types of schools and training centers
specifically designed to breed a reliable
elite. In addition, a new organization
has been set up which no German boy
between ten and eighteen, and no girl
between ten and twenty-one, can escape.
A brief glance at the origins of this
organization comprising the whole German youth, the Hitler Youth, as it is
officially called, will show its essential
aims and characteristics.

The Hitler Youth was founded in
1926. From its inception the membership and leadership of the Nazi party
had a proportionately larger number of
young people below the age of thirty
than any other German party. One of
the factors that doomed the Republic
was its inability to provide the German
youth with substitutes for the traditional

attractions of militarism and the emotional appeal of the uniform. The flock-
ing of the German youth into the Nazi
party when it could freely choose its allegiance showed that the Nazis were better
able than other parties to satisfy the
longing for military discipline and
subordination at a time when the army
had to be limited to the relatively small
size dictated by the Allied powers at
Versailles. . . .

Two executive orders of March 25,
1939, introduced two new and revolutionary principles into the status of
German youth between ten and eighteen:
first, the youth service duty (*Jugend-
dienstpflicht*) ; and second, the youth
arrest and youth service arrest (*Jugen-
darrest, Jugenddienstarrest*) . This is the
only case known in the history of
ancient or modern totalitarian systems
in which children, boys and girls, from
the age of ten upward are subject to
compulsory service for the state, and are
subject to imprisonment for violation of
their duties. . . .

The youth service duty is now put on
an equal basis with compulsory school
attendance. Parents who influence their
children to abstain from this new service
duty are punishable by law, and their
children may be taken away from their
homes and put into orphans' homes or
with other families. Hundreds of families have already been punished for
exercising a bad influence on their children. The latter are encouraged to de-
nounce their parents to their teachers
or Hitler Youth leaders, often the same
persons. The youth service duty for the
children from ten to eighteen, both boys
and girls, is frankly compared by a Nazi
writer and expert in the field, to the
compulsory military service of the adults.

BURTON H. KLEIN (1917–   ) is a distinguished
economic analyst whose study of Hitler's war
preparations grew out of work he did on the
United States Strategic Bombing Survey. He
subsequently served on the Council of Economic
Advisers to President Eisenhower, and is presently
head of the economics department of The RAND
Corporation. In this selection, Klein concludes
that Nazi ideology had little effect on Nazi economic
practices and that Hitler did not make preparations
for a great war of conquest. In dealing with the
problem of preparations for war, what factors other
than the economic issue discussed by Klein might
also be considered? Does evidence that Hitler
was not fully prepared for a war of conquest
preclude the possibility that he nevertheless
gambled on winning such a war? *

The Economy Not Designed for War

When Germany marched against Poland in September, 1939, her military might was not questioned. The Nazi government, it was commonly believed, had for six years concentrated the country's resources on preparation for war. This was a tacit assumption of the diplomacy of the period, and a point of major emphasis in the voluminous writings on Germany.

Nearly all the economic and political studies of prewar Germany agreed on three major propositions: (1) that in the period before 1939 Germany had succeeded in building up a military machine whose comparative strength was enormous; (2) that a substantial part of the increase in production from the low level of the depression was channeled into the construction of a huge war potential; (3) that all economic considerations were subordinated to the central task of preparing for war. . . .

Even a cursory examination of the official German data recently made available shows that the validity of these propositions is questionable. . . .

In the prewar period, the German economy produced both "butter" and "guns"—much more of the former and much less of the latter than has been commonly assumed. By 1937, civilian consumption, investment in consumer goods industries, and government non-war expenditures equalled or exceeded previous peak levels. There is no ques-

* Reprinted by permission of the publishers from Burton H. Klein, *Germany's Economic Preparation for War*, Cambridge, Mass.: Harvard University Press, Copyright, 1959, by the President and Fellows of Harvard College. Pp. 1, 76-82.

tion, therefore, of a rearmament program so large that it prevented a substantial recovery of civilian production.

The volume of expenditures for rearmament was actually quite modest. In the period 1933 through 1938 rearmament expenditures absorbed less than 10 per cent of Germany's gross national product, and even as late as 1938, only 15 per cent. The volume of munitions production and the number of divisions which Germany mobilized was, by comparison with published appraisal, small. Investment in those industries comprising the war potential was not much larger than the volume reached in the prosperous years of the previous decade and was small in relation to total investment.

The review of Germany's raw material preparations for war shows that at the time the Nazis came into power Germany was not self-sufficient in such important materials as iron ore, ferroalloys, oil, copper, rubber, aluminum, bauxite, and foodstuffs. Of these, only in foodstuffs and rubber did the Germans attain a substantial degree of self-sufficiency prior to the war. They found it impossible to become independent of foreign sources for such important materials as copper ores, bauxite, and ferroalloys because Germany lacked the basic resources. For other important raw materials, notably iron ore and synthetic oil, the self-sufficiency programs were largely unsuccessful because they were begun too late and were inadequately implemented.

Raw material distribution controls were largely unsuccessful in increasing the flow of raw materials into the war sector of the economy. Priorities and allocation schemes were applied to only a few commodities and in those cases where they were used they were largely ineffective.

The stockpiling program also did little to improve Germany's raw material position. At the beginning of the war such important materials as gasoline, rubber, iron ore, copper ore, and bauxite were in sufficient supply for less than six months of estimated needs. After this period Germany's current output of these materials could cover only a fraction of stated requirements. The weakness of Germany's raw material position at the beginning of the war was recognized both by Hitler and by the German General Staff.

Concerning Germany's mobilization of manpower, the Nazis increased their total labor supply only insofar as they eliminated unemployment. A larger percentage of the population was not taken into the labor force, working hours were increased only slightly, and labor efficiency in industry was not, in general, improved. Second, . . . the Nazis did not shift a large proportion of the labor force into war activities. The only two major changes in the distribution of the labor force between 1925 and 1939 were a decline in agricultural employment and an increase in public employment. The shrinkage in the agricultural labor force was contradictory to Nazi policy. A large increase in the army from the 100,000 limit set by the Treaty of Versailles is hardly surprising. What is surprising, however, is the fact that the relative size of the industrial labor force was no greater in 1939 than in 1925, and that the relative numbers engaged in civilian production hardly declined.

On the basis of these observations it [is] concluded that there was no real mobilization of manpower prior to the outbreak of war.

Thus, whether we examine the general nature of the German economic recovery, or the raw material self-sufficiency program, or the mobilization of manpower, the same general conclusion is evident: The scale of Germany's economic mobilization for war was quite modest.

A number of reasons [may be] given why the rearmament was not, in general or in special aspects, on a larger scale.

A basic reason why the Germans did not have a rearmament on the scale popularly assumed is simply that their war plans did not require such a large effort. . . . Hitler hoped to satisfy his territorial ambitions in a piecemeal fashion; he hoped to conquer each enemy so speedily that the democracies would not have time to intervene, and to have a breathing space after each conquest during which preparations could be made for the next. There is no doubt that this type of strategy called for less massive preparations than one involving a prolonged struggle against a coalition of major powers.

While this blitzkrieg strategy explains why Germany did not undertake preparations on an enormous scale, it cannot explain why they were not at least moderately larger. In the first place, while Hitler hoped not to get involved in a major war, he did not dismiss that possibility. Moreover, there is ample evidence that both he and the General Staff wanted a larger economic effort.

This was prevented by a variety of factors, consideration of which yields four principal reasons why the German rearmament was not, in fact, larger. The first and probably the most important reason is that the government was unwilling to increase public expenditures and incur larger deficits. A larger deficit, it was thought, would destroy confidence in the currency and lead to inflation. This fear of inflation was a major factor in explaining economic policy of the pre-Nazi governments. It played an important role in determining

Nazi policy for economic recovery, and it was a restraining influence on both total military expenditures and the development of Germany's raw material industries. There is no doubt that without this concern about inflation, and without such an effective exponent of financial conservatism as Schacht, Germany would have had a larger rearmament.

The second reason was the unwillingness of the Germans to surrender a part of their prosperity level of consumption. The government's disinclination to ask for civilian sacrifices was demonstrated in a number of instances. One of these was its refusal to consider higher taxes as an alternative to deficit spending; another was its unwillingness in 1937 to cut food imports in favor of increased raw material imports; still another was its failure to transfer workers out of unessential occupations.

Until 1936, rearmament and increased civilian consumption could be achieved simultaneously by drawing on unemployed resources. Indeed, the rearmament deficits had a stimulating effect on consumption. There was no conflict, therefore, in having both more "butter" and more "guns." In the years 1937 and 1938, however, the German economy was operating at near full employment, and a sizable increase in armament expenditures could have been achieved only at the expense of some decline in civilian consumption. It would have required at least a sharp curtailment of some types of civilian goods production, notably consumer durables and residential construction. It appears, however, that the German government was unwilling to ask for such sacrifices.

It must be admitted that even if the above factors limited the amount of resources available for war preparations, the size of these preparations to some extent was dependent on the efficiency with which the program was directed. Nazi inefficiency in planning and carrying out their war production program is the third reason why war preparations were not larger. Note, for example, the manner in which the various branches of the armed forces procured their material. It is a first principle of war economy that competition between the branches of the armed forces for supplies is not the most efficient method of procurement; this was learned in World War I. Yet, . . . before the outbreak of war there was no central agency which examined and coordinated the material demands of the German army, navy, and air force.

The review of Germany's raw material preparations for war [shows] a lack of efficiency in both the planning and execution of the program. In drawing up the plans the idea of attaining a balanced program seems to have been given little consideration. As a result the planned production of some commodities was ample, if not excessive, for wartime requirements, while for others it was not nearly sufficient. Once drawn up, the adequacy of the measures taken to implement the various plans was not solely a matter of their importance. The iron ore and synthetic oil programs were designated by Hitler as top priority projects; yet it was in these fields that Germany's preparations were most deficient. The Nazi prewar experience with raw material distribution controls is another example of inefficient economic administration. A steel priority system was instituted in 1937, yet by 1941 an effective method still had not been found.

Something else which makes us suspicious of Nazi economic organizational ability is the composition of their governmental expenditures. Given the difficulty of increasing public outlays, and assuming that preparations for war had priority over other governmental activities, it follows that the latter should have been cut to an absolute minimum. But . . . public nonwar expenditures in 1937 and 1938 were much above any previous peak. Especially prominent in the German budget were expenditures on highway construction, municipal improvements, and party buildings.

In the light of such evidence, it would be difficult to deny that a more rational and better executed program would have given the Nazis larger rearmament.

The fourth reason why war preparations were not larger was that Hitler was unable to subordinate various vested and emerging interests to his central task of preparing for war. One of these interests was the Nazi party itself. The opposition of this group made it difficult to cut public nonwar expenditures. When Schacht attempted to cut expenditures for municipal improvements, he was invariably opposed by some prominent party members. When, on numerous occasions, he tried to reduce the budget of the German Labor Front, the issue was taken to Hitler, who invariably decided in favor of the latter. Because it was contradictory to its ideology, the party also opposed measures to force a larger number of women into the labor force.

The German industrialists were another group whose interests could not be disregarded. In our account of Germany's iron and steel-expansion program, we showed that the interests of the steel cartel conflicted with those of the state; that the industrialists refused to carry out the program themselves; that they strongly voiced their opposition to the government's undertaking of the project; and that eventually the government had to drop its elaborate plans for expansion of iron ore and steel capacity.

Part of the government's reluctance for incurring large deficits may have been the concern that they would destroy the confidence of the industrialists in the regime and hence their cooperation in rearmament. Certainly there was little ground for fearing that moderately larger deficits would have led to a runaway price inflation. For by 1936 Germany had adequate machinery for controlling wages and prices; this was demonstrated during the war when, in spite of enormous government outlays and deficits by prewar standards, prices increased very little.

An adequate account of the importance of pressure groups in Nazi Germany will have to wait the studies of political scientists who were close to the situation. When such studies are made, it is likely that it will be found that the resistance of particular groups to Hitler's aims, for one reason or another, was as effective in circumscribing the German war potential as a lack of iron ore or oil.

The contrast between the conclusions reached in this summary of Germany's economic preparations for war and those of earlier studies should be reemphasized.

That the Nazis were undertaking massive preparations for war was the central assumption of practically all political and economic writings on Nazi Germany. In achieving this end, it was supposed that only money and not resources mattered to the Germans, that the civilian population as well as various private interests were compelled to make large sacrifices, and that the government was super-efficient in directing the program.

Actually, Germany's rearmament was on a much smaller scale than was generally assumed and it did not involve a large drain of resources from the civilian economy. The factors which prevented the Nazis from having a larger rearmament were, first, the fear of larger deficits; second, the government's unwillingness to ask for civilian sacrifices; third, Hitler's inability to subordinate various private interests to his aims; and, finally, a lack of efficiency in the direction of the program. Even without these restraining influences, however, it is unlikely that Germany would have made the tremendous preparations with which she was credited. Such an economic effort was not required by Hitler's strategy.

The following selection is taken from the most authoritative, comprehensive, and detailed study yet written on Hitler's methods in consolidating his dictatorship. WOLFGANG SAUER (1920–   ), a specialist in military history, has been a research fellow of the Institute for Political Science of the Free University of Berlin and a visiting professor at the University of California at Berkeley. Sauer argues that Hitler deliberately plotted a great war of conquest in eastern Europe—even at the risk of a general European war. Indeed, war was absolutely essential to Hitler's economic plans. Is it possible to reconcile the interpretations of Klein and Sauer? Do the two authors draw their conclusions from similar evidence?*

The Economy Geared to War

It has long been recognized that in *Mein Kampf* Hitler set forth grandiose plans for military aggression, particularly toward the East. But the absurdity of his ideas, . . . and especially what seemed at first glance to be the confused character of National Socialist foreign policy up to 1938, prompted uninformed contemporaries, as well as scholarly investigators since 1945, to question the relevance of Hitler's early statements to his later policy. . . . There can now no longer be any doubt that Hitler always kept firmly in view the ideas for military aggression which he had developed in *Mein Kampf* during the mid-twenties.

The sources and motives from which these ideas sprang were . . . of a very diverse nature. Their ideological presuppositions . . . were clearly an amalgam in which older Great German, Pan-German concepts and the idea of *Mitteleuropa* were combined with Haushofer's geopolitical pseudo-theories and placed against a background of nationalism and imperialism. As the framework for his ideas, Hitler utilized the social Darwinian concept of struggle for existence, which served to justify his demand for adequate living space.

In its essentials, all this is already known. What has not been sufficiently noted until now, however, is that Hitler's theory also . . . included an economic

* From Wolfgang Sauer "Die Mobilmachung der Gewalt" in Karl Dietrich Bracher, Wolfgang Sauer, and Gerhard Schulz, *Die nationalsozialistische Machtergreifung: Studien zur Errichtung des totalitären Herrschaftssystems in Deutschland 1933/34* (Cologne, 1960), pp. 744–764. Translated by Robert G. L. Waite. The Yale University Press, which will publish a translation of the entire volume, has granted permission for use of the translation which appears here.

policy. The policy was, in essence, to postpone fundamental economic and political decisions pending the acquisition of living space and to bridge the interim with stop-gap measures. This economic policy inevitably brought Hitler's government into a steadily sharpening crisis in the face of which war finally became the unavoidable solution. War would have been the outcome of this policy even if the Nazi leaders had been prepared to sacrifice ideological postulates to a more realistic approach to foreign policy.

It is therefore precisely the economic and political aspects of the Nazi ideology . . . which afford an excellent point of departure for discussing Hitler's ideas on war—ideas which at the outset were capricious but which were gradually transformed by their own internal dynamics into a fateful pattern permitting him no retreat even had he wanted it. . . .

Let us begin with a brief consideration of Hitler's statements in *Mein Kampf*. As early as this [1924–25] social Darwinism occupied the central place in Hitler's thinking. . . . The conception of life as a perpetual fight with everyone against everyone else—be it individuals, or groups, or nations—constitutes the one comprehensible theme leading through the amorphous, self-contradictory agglomeration of half-baked ideas displayed here as the National Socialist "world view." Indeed, for the sake of Darwinian struggle, even racism—otherwise extolled as the revolutionary new showpiece of National Socialist ideology—was at times unceremoneously pushed aside. . . .

Thus the principle of struggle for existence clearly took precedence over race; moreover it becomes obvious that Hitler was not (as is so often said) referring only to the struggle among na-

tions, but also to the struggles between individuals. . . . What merits special emphasis here is Hitler's conviction that this elemental battle with everyone against everyone was "eternal" . . . and that whoever did not prevail in this fight would be destroyed: "who rests, rusts." This line of reasoning led him to the concept that the security and successful growth of nations lay exclusively in an expansion which was both geographic and ethnic. He therefore fulminated against birth control, which would condemn the German people to "extinction," and at the same time insisted that he could assure the German people's existence "for hundreds of years hence" if only sufficient "ground and soil" were conquered.

This demand for the conquest of living space also constituted . . . Hitler's economic policy—or what was supposed to pass for economic policy. Actually, there was for Hitler only one relevant question with respect to economic policy: . . . how to meet the threat of starvation which would result from the steady growth of population in a constant amount of living space. He discussed four possible solutions: (1) birth control, (2) "internal colonization" . . . (3) the acquisition of new territory, and (4) industrialization with exports and a colonial policy. . . . [Hitler concluded that] the third way was the only feasible solution . . . and he thought of the East, especially of Russia. "We National Socialists," so ran his oft-quoted formula, "will stop the eternal movement of Germans to southern and western Europe and turn our gaze to land in the East."

It was clear to Hitler that such a policy could not possibly be fulfilled without war, but he incorporated it without scruple into his plans: "What is denied to good will must be seized by your fist." Finally, he said that the acquisition of land for colonization . . . could be achieved only with bloodshed, but the goal must be worth the bloodshed. . . .

People have often noticed and criticized Hitler's dilettantism and ignorance in economic matters. But . . . there was a system behind his pose: the system of eliminating facts and stressing one fixed idea which ultimately—explicitly or not —pointed only to war. This process and its result are shown with great clarity in the speech he made to the army commanders at the beginning of February 1933 [a few days after he had seized power]. . . .

Since this speech represents a significant stage in the development of Hitler's thinking, we will examine it rather closely. He began by using his favorite rhetorical device of those days and painted a somber picture: His government was confronted by enormous, almost unsolvable, problems and was consequently forced to bring about a complete transformation of internal political conditions. He then discussed in detail the economic crisis and the unemployment situation. After an unsuccessful attempt to analyze both problems, he set forth his solution, in the course of which he let fall completely all the screens that had cloaked his remarks [on other occasions]. . . . He said that the only solution [to the economic crisis] lay in a land settlement policy which would harness the army of unemployed, but this was only a temporary emergency measure because the living space for such a policy remained too small. Only when living space had been adequately expanded could one count on a complete solution. Expansion could take place in two directions: either in the acquisition of new markets for German products or—much better—through the conquest and ruthless Germanization of new living space to the East. In any event,

it was certain that present economic conditions could be improved only by war.

This is obviously nothing but application of the theory in *Mein Kampf* to the concrete situation. . . .

The importance of this speech is further emphasized by an address Hitler gave at the Defense Ministry about a year later, on February 28, 1934, before approximately the same circle of military commanders, with the addition of a group of high SA and SS leaders, including Göring and Röhm. . . . Once again he began with contrived pessimism: "The German people are confronted by frightful misery." To be sure, he said, the NSDAP [Nazi Party][1] has already solved the unemployment problem (an assertion which was, to say the least, a bold one), but within about eight years, when the public works program will have been completed, a really serious economic recession will set in. . . .This evil, he continued, can be alleviated only by finding new living space for the excess German population. And—since the Western powers will not assume the role of placid spectators—"brief, decisive blows first against the West and then against the East will be necessary." These observations, reproduced here in abbreviated form, clearly must be understood to mean—as later speeches show— that by "blows" against the West Hitler meant a war of containment against the Western powers, especially France, while the actual expansion would be toward the East. . . .

As will be shown presently, [Hitler] spurred on rearmament by all possible means and cut off possible retreat from the rearmament program by linking it with his solution to the economic crisis. In 1936, when he had passed the point of no return, he recklessly accepted the consequences. Evidence of this is to be

[1] See above, p. 9.

found in his memorandum implementing the Four Year Plan of 1936. . . .

Even people who were not aware of Hitler's earlier statements about his war aims must have been hit between the eyes by the fact that this memorandum was not concerned with a program for peaceful development of a self-sufficient economy. It was concerned with preparations for war. . . . In fact, Hitler's entire argument focused on war: "If we don't succeed in the shortest possible time in making the German army . . . the best army in the world, Germany will be lost!" The idea that rearmament had to be delayed in order to free foreign exchange for the stockpiling of raw materials "rests on a total misunderstanding . . . of the tasks and military requirements lying ahead of us." It is now essential, he said, to secure "the food requirements for peace and above all the materials for war." A solution of the fuel problem is mandatory, not only for peacetime progress in motorization and industrialization but "for the coming war effort." And finally, "the existence of the national economy and above all the requirements of the war effort must not become dependent upon the necessity of importing ore." . . .

Hitler's Four Year Plan memorandum . . . has sometimes been cited as evidence of his incompetence and ignorance in economic questions. These deficiencies seem to be revealed with extraordinary clarity in two principal ways: first, the memorandum contains demands which . . . could not conceivably be fulfilled; second, Hitler's ideas about a war economy apparently proceeded from erroneous assumptions. But analysis of his arguments leads to the unexpected conclusion that such criticism misses the whole point. Hitler knew well the objections of the experts and was quite capable of following their line of rea-

soning. If he disregarded their proposals, he did so because they did not provide the solutions he wanted. . . . They . . . did not go deeply enough for Hitler. They merely offered temporary solutions and guaranteed him neither complete security against economic crises nor the total autarchy he was striving for. . . . Above everything else, they made him dependent—dependent on the laws of the free market, especially of the world market, on its currency, on association with trading partners—and furthermore, the plans of the experts presupposed consideration for competitors. But Hitler did not want to trade; he did not even want to negotiate. He wanted to give orders. He therefore demanded a "final solution for the future" which would be brought about by "political leadership" and which would "someday" solve once and for all Germany's economic problems through the expansion of living space.

The interim period was to be bridged over with stop-gap measures that would satisfy the minimum requirements for food and consumer goods and provide a maximum of war materials for achieving the "final solution." . . .

The decisive aspect of his transitional solution, which has until now not been sufficiently recognized, is that it entailed the *deliberate* renunciation of all consideration of basic economic laws. Up to 1936 the German economy had been reasonably able to satisfy the demands that the National Socialist system, especially the armament program, had placed upon it, and it had done so without requiring sacrifice of the normal operational procedures and the essential laws governing economic life. But in the process the economy had reached the limits of its capabilities. Now, in 1936, further advance was possible only if one of two courses were taken: either

Germany could return to a normal economy operating within the general framework of the world economy, or Germany could be forced to accept completely a ruthless, aggressive plunder economy [*Raubbauwirtschaft*] which denied all principles of economics. Obviously only very slow progress could be expected if the first way were chosen. Indeed, Hitler feared quite rightly that this course would not bring him sufficient power to overwhelm his adversaries. . . . Expansionist plans such as Hitler's could not possibly be carried out under a normal economic system.

But Hitler had no intention of being forced to make a choice. Trusting in his "intuition" and highly suspicious of rationality in any form, he took his chances and gambled that his plans for "living space" would be achieved by capitalizing on the inferiority in arms of the Western powers . . . and by exploiting to the extreme every available resource in Germany. In this way he would gain the initial superiority that would enable him to eliminate one opponent and then another in surprise "short jabs" after first carefully isolating them. . . . This was the program he had planned as early as 1934. . . .

If Hitler deliberately contemplated such an extreme overextension of Germany's economic strength in peacetime, how did he imagine the economy of Germany could be conducted in time of war? In this area, too, his critics—contemporary as well as later—have insisted that one simply cannot conduct a war with an economy that has been bled so white —one as exhausted as that which Hitler contemplated. But here again critics underestimated Hitler's intelligence and his ruthlessness. He was not blind to the problem, but he believed he had ways of solving it and could disregard the advice of the experts. . . .

[His plan was simple:] the conquered countries would pay for German war preparations as well as for the German war effort. Hitler's Four Year Plan deliberately risked the total ruin of Germany's economy in the expectation that it would be built up again by means of a war which would serve as a gigantic plundering foray. In the same way the difficulties of economic mobilization which could not be overcome during peacetime would be solved by war. . . .

In 1936, when Hitler committed himself to the plunder economy of the Four Year Plan, he committed himself also to starting a war in the near future, if his economic policy were not to end in catastrophe. And the war forced him, in turn, to adopt a policy of looting the conquered areas which deprived him of any possibility of pursuing a reasonable, sane occupation policy. "This policy of plunder which ran counter to all political sense," writes Hans Buchheim, "[was] the logical consequence of the decision which Hitler took in 1936 to include even in his war plans the economic potential of the territories which still remained to be conquered. . . ." That was the policy of the reckless gambler: "Double or Nothing!" "Victory or Disaster!"

The military and diplomatic counterpart of the economic program of 1936 was set forth in Hitler's well-known statements at the meeting with his military commanders on November 5 ,1937, and preserved as the Hossbach Memorandum. At this time Hitler ordered economic mobilization and gave his commanders the following task: "The German army . . . and the German economy must be ready for war within four years." Hitler then began . . . to plan concrete ways of starting and carrying through the war of conquest he required. . . .

He reiterated his conclusion that "the single remedy—one which to us perhaps seems like a dream—[lies] in winning greater living space in Europe." To be sure, he admitted, one must reckon on the resistance of our two "archenemies" [*Hassgegner*], England and France. Thus he had now given up hope of an alliance with England, which had originally been the cornerstone of his plans for expansion. . . . After he had analyzed the geopolitical situation of England and France, he finally came to the conclusion that "only force can solve the German question and that is never without risk. . . ."

These observations show the undeviating development of Hitler's mania for living space, and the statements that follow reflect the pressure which had resulted since 1936 from his policy of excessive military and economic rearmament. There are, he said, three possible ways of achieving a solution by force: one will occur if Germany is forced to attack at the latest by 1943–45; one of the other two alternatives will occur if an earlier attack is possible. But why, according to Hitler, was the period 1943–45 the extreme time limit? Because—as the Führer answered—"after this time . . . we can only expect a change to our disadvantage." . . . Rearmament could not be significantly increased; arms and munitions would become obsolescent; "special weapons" could not be concealed indefinitely; an increase in the numbers of those men in older recruitment years could not be expected; and—in the face of the increasing armament of "the outside world"—Germany's position would become "relatively weaker." . . . Finally, the fact had to be faced that "the party and its leaders were growing older." In other words, the armament advantage which would have been forced out of the German economy by ruthless pressure

would be endangered; economic catastrophe would be on the horizon; and Hitler's increasing age would steadily diminish his chances of proving his military genius "to all history." . . .

The pressure of time which Hitler already felt acutely was alluded to once again shortly [after the November 1937 conference]. Foreign Minister von Neurath, who had been "extremely shocked" by Hitler's statements, demanded a showdown with him and in January 1938 argued "that his policy would inevitably lead to world war." Neurath said that he could not associate himself with such a policy. "Many of [Hitler's] plans could be effected by peaceful means, to be sure somewhat more slowly. Whereupon Hitler told me he had no more time."

That was precisely the point: Hitler could wait no longer. He had started the game and he had to keep on playing. These statements show his determination to carry out his insane plan; and they also show that in his eyes the Munich Agreement of September 1938 was only a partial victory, for it blocked the path to war, which was the last avenue of escape from the crisis he had created.

Peace was not Hitler's only worry. For in the course of the Czech crisis it had become evident that the German people showed none of the enthusiasm for war which he needed for his plans. His reaction to the people's attitude is reflected in a recently discovered recording of the speech he delivered to the German press in the Braunhaus in Munich on November 10, 1938. The speech was made barely forty-eight hours after the infamous "National Crystal Night"—the first organized mass terror action perpetrated by the Nazi regime against the Jews. Simple souls might have thought Hitler had called the press in an effort to justify the atrocities. He had no such thing in mind. He did not even mention directly the events of November 8–9. Perhaps he equated them with those "little things" which he contrasted to the "great tasks" and "miraculous accomplishments" of his government. Such things as the atrocities, in his mind, sank "into insignificant absurdities . . . when measured against the mighty deeds I perform." And he insisted that "nobody talks any more about it, so I too can forget all about it. It isn't noticed any more. Nobody sees it."

If one could believe that Adolf Hitler had a conscience, one would have to assume that this repeated affirmation was an attempt to quiet it. But perhaps that is assuming too much. In any event, Hitler was concerned with very different matters in this speech. His oratorical efforts were directed not to the justification—however threadbare—of an atrocity, but to preparing the way for a new atrocity which would far surpass any that had gone before.

That his audience consisted of representatives of the press may explain why he did not set forth his war plans with the chilling candor he had used a year before in addressing his military commanders. He even began innocuously by thanking the press for the support given him in the achievements of the previous year. Then he let the mask fall, and the rest of his speech had only two themes: his badly concealed disappointment, fury, and anxiety over the "defeatist" attitude of the people and, as a corollary theme, emphatic orders to the press to mold public opinion into enthusiasm for war. His bitterness over the silent opposition of the German people to his war policy knew no bounds and mounted to passionate hatred when he referred to the experts and critics from the circle of "the upper ten thousand," whom he reviled as "this inbred,

intellectual and hysterical stratum." He blamed them for the widespread defeatism . . . and hurled a threat: "When I look at that intellectual strata in our midst, well, we need them, unfortunately. Otherwise we could some day . . . oh, I don't know, wipe them out or something like that. But unfortunately we need them. . . ." The transcription of the phonograph record indicates "Excitement" in the auditorium at this point. . . .

Oddly enough, Hitler felt slightly to blame for the situation. He recognized that the task of making a people warminded "could not be accomplished . . . in one or two years." Consequently, it should have been begun earlier . . . but unfortunately that had not been possible because "conditions forced me *for decades* [sic] to speak almost solely about peace." Only by doing so had it been possible "to give the German people . . . the armament which is always the necessary precondition for the next step." . . .

But, he continued, this restraint is no longer necessary. On the one hand, the tune of sweet reasonableness which was played during the Czech crisis—in which propagandistic and psychological preparations "had to be carried out for the first time to the nth degree"—failed in its effect both on our own people and on foreigners. "In any case, I believe that this record, this pacifist record, has run down." On the other hand, *these decades* [sic] of active peace propaganda have also had their very "regrettable consequences." They have increased the peoples' longing for peace and deceived them about their leaders' true intentions.

In Hitler's own words—as well as in his style—the danger was thus created "that the German nation, instead of being armed to meet events, is filled instead with a spirit which in the long run would bring defeatism and would, and would have to, ruin the successes of the present government." It was the task of the German press to clear this obstacle from the path of his war plans. Here he came to the second principle point which reveals the purpose of the entire meeting: he gave orders to the press to strengthen the psychological preparation for war. Again and again and with rising emphasis he told the press that it must prepare the still reluctant German people for the coming war. . . . He said flatly that although the press was obviously not supposed to talk about force "as such," nevertheless it was necessary "to explain certain foreign events to the German people in such a way that the inner voice of the people will itself cry out for force." To attain this end . . . "the self-consciousness of the people must be strengthened step by step by every possible means." Germans, he concluded, must learn "to believe fanatically in final victory" and must be ready "to stand firm even when thunder rolls and lightning flashes." In short, "the entire nation must stand behind the Führer as one disciplined army. . . ."

A similar tone was maintained . . . in the three speeches of 1939 to his military commanders in which Hitler explained his decision to go to war. In general they were very like the earlier military speeches. His guiding thought kept recurring with enervating monotony: social Darwinism, living space, dangerous historical comparisons. . . . One finds only three specific observations of interest: (1) Hitler had to admit that his original plan to isolate his real or imaginary enemies and crush them one by one no longer had any real chance of success; consequently the danger of a European, yes even a world war, threatened. (2) In spite of that, Hitler

was now irrevocably determined to find a pretext for this war which he had sought for so long. (3) He had decided against his original intention—to make the first attack against Poland. . . .

Particularly in the first two prewar speeches, the contradiction clearly appeared that Hitler wanted to unleash the war even though the preconditions in foreign affairs which he himself had originally demanded did not exist. As early as in *Mein Kampf* he had insisted on the basic principle that the eastward expansion . . . could take place only in alliance with England and after the defeat of France. And as late as November 5, 1937—long after an alliance with England was outside the range of possibility—he still demanded that England at least remain neutral. But now, on May 23, 1939, he announced that he was prepared to launch a war even if he had to fight simultaneously against Poland, England, and France: "The basic principle to be observed in our conflict with Poland—which will begin with an attack against Poland—is that we will succeed only if the West stays out of the game; but if that isn't possible, then it is better to attack the West and Poland at the same time."

Thus not only the psychological preconditions but also the conditions in foreign affairs which his "genius" had previously required had now become illusory. And the real reason that drove him onward emerged all the more strongly from the jungle of Hitlerian argument. He declared point-blank that the tactics of bluff were now obsolete: "Further success can no longer be attained without bloodshed. . . . We can't expect a repeat of Czechoslovakia." What successes, then, did he still require—this creator of "Greater Germany," this "most successful German statesman since Bismarck?" He answered the question himself: "The eighty million Germans have solved the problem of ideology; now they must solve the economic problem. Not a single German will be able to avoid creating these economic preconditions. . . . It is not possible to solve the problem unless we invade foreign countries and attack foreign property [!] . . . One can let things drift for a certain length of time but then it becomes necessary to solve our problems one way or another. The choice is between rise or fall. . . ."

Thus even if the situation at the time was not yet directly threatening, it would be shortly, as Hitler correctly forsaw, unless he could save his regime by attacking "foreign property." War as a war of plunder, a fantastic concept that Hitler derived from an alleged "law of history," . . . had now become, in the critical moment of a frivolously begun game, the only salvation for Germany.

It was a salvation that would cost Germany and the world millions of dead and crippled. . . . But it offered one great advantage to Hitler. War gave him his only chance of maintaining himself in power, and it enticed him with the prospect of going down in history as "the greatest military commander of all time." Under these conditions it was not at all difficult for the Führer to make his decision: "It is usually hard to make decisions which must lead to bloodshed, but it is relatively easy for us to do so in this case because there is for us really only one choice: victory or defeat."

In the year 1939, he still had an advantage in armament over his enemies, and he was determined to make use of it. "The time is now more propitious than in two or three years," he announced in August. . . . Thus the bathos of his "all or nothing"—so often shrugged off as mere theatrical pose—suddenly took on a frightful reality. Already in May he had declared unequivocally: "The hope that we can win cheaply is a dangerous hope. There is no such possibility. It is a matter of life or death." And again in August: "For us there exists only the alternative of striking or being destroyed." Finally, in November: "Every hope for compromise is childish. Victory or defeat! . . . I have to choose between victory or destruction. I choose victory."

But what would happen if fate were against him? Was it not to be taken into account that the entire German people would be drawn along with him into the destruction he prophesied? Hitler had two answers to this question. One of them had already been given in his speech to the press in 1938. Here he had sought to amuse his audience with a cynical jest. Since Roman times, he said, the German people have lived through many wars and catastrophes, "they have survived a world war and a revolution—they will even survive me!" The other answer, equally cynical but more a part of Hitler's basic logic, is implied in his statement of November, 1939 [after his victory over Poland]: "The issue is not the existence of National Socialist Germany but rather who will dominate Europe in the future. . . ."

For Hitler, war had become . . . the *conditio sine qua non* for the development of the National Socialist economic program. In proclaiming from the outset that he wanted war, he was not merely indulging in an outburst of bloodthirsty fantasy; rather, he was setting forth the goal which was as necessary as it was reprehensible—a goal which was the logical consequence of his rejection of the existing economic system.

A point of focus for discussion of Nazism in practice is provided by A. J. P. TAYLOR's influential interpretation of Hitler and the causes of World War II. Taylor insists that all other historians have misunderstood Hitler, misinterpreted his motives, misread his words, and misjudged his foreign policy. Hitler was no fanatic; he was an opportunist. He did not really mean what he said; he spoke for effect. He did not plan a war; it was thrust upon him. Taylor is a persuasive writer. And—in spite of his penchant for paradox and *gaminerie*—he is also a deeply reflective one. He requires close reading and hard questioning. How valid is this interpretation of Hitler's personality? What part did Hitler's beliefs play in the conduct of his foreign policy? Is Taylor justified in implying that Hitler's foreign policy can be discussed without reference to his domestic practices? In what ways does Klein support Taylor's thesis? On what issues and for what reasons does Sauer disagree with Taylor?*

► Hitler: A "Traditional" German Statesman

Hitler was appointed Chancellor by President Hindenburg in a strictly constitutional way and for solidly democratic reasons. Whatever ingenious speculators, liberal or Marxist, might say, Hitler was not made Chancellor because he would help the German capitalists to destroy the trade unions, nor because he would give the German generals a great army, still less a great war. He was appointed because he and his Nationalist allies could provide a majority in the Reichstag, and thus end the anomalous four years of government by presidential decree. He was not expected to carry through revolutionary changes in either home or foreign affairs. . . . In one sphere alone he changed nothing. His foreign policy was that of his predecessors, of the professional diplomats at the foreign ministry, and indeed of virtually all Germans. Hitler, too, wanted to free Germany from the restrictions of the peace treaty; to restore a great German army; and then to make Germany the greatest power in Europe from her natural weight. There were occasional differences in emphasis. . . . But the general pattern was unchanged.

This is not the accepted view. Writ-

* From *The Origins of the Second World War* by A. J. P. Taylor. Copyright © 1961 by A .J. P. Taylor. Reprinted by permission of Atheneum Publishers and Hamish Hamilton Ltd. Pp. 67–72, 131–134, 142–146, 148–153, 166–167, 187, 189, 192–193, 201–204, 210–211, 215–219, 248–251, 262–264, 272–278.

ers of great authority have seen in Hitler a system-maker, deliberately preparing from the first a great war which would destroy existing civilisation and make him master of the world. In my opinion, statesmen are too absorbed by events to follow a preconceived plan. They take one step, and the next follows from it. The systems are created by historians, as happened with Napoleon; and the systems attributed to Hitler are really those of Hugh Trevor-Roper, Elizabeth Wiskemann, and Alan Bullock. There is some ground for these speculations. Hitler was himself an amateur historian, or rather a generaliser on history; and he created systems in his spare time. These systems were day-dreams. Chaplin grasped this, with an artist's genius, when he showed the Great Dictator transforming the world into a toy balloon and kicking it to the ceiling with the point of his toe. Hitler always saw himself, in these day-dreams, as master of the world. But the world which he dreamt to master and the way he would do it changed with changing circumstances. *Mein Kampf* was written in 1925, under the impact of the French occupation of the Ruhr. Hitler dreamt then of destroying French supremacy in Europe; and the method was to be alliance with Italy and Great Britain. His *Table Talk* was delivered far in occupied territory, during the campaign against Soviet Russia; and then Hitler dreamt of some fantastic Empire which would rationalise his career of conquest. His final legacy was delivered from the Bunker, when he was on the point of suicide; it is not surprising that he transformed this into a doctrine of universal destruction. Academic ingenuity has discovered in these pronouncements the disciple of Nietzsche, the geopolitician, or the emulator of Attila. I hear in them only the generalisations of a powerful,

but uninstructed, intellect; dogmas which echo the conversation of any Austrian café or German beer-house.

There was one element of system in Hitler's foreign policy, though it was not new. His outlook was "continental," as Stresemann's had been before him. Hitler did not attempt to revive the "World Policy" which Germany had pursued before 1914; he made no plans for a great battle-fleet; he did not parade a grievance over the lost colonies, except as a device for embarrassing the British; he was not even interested in the Middle East—hence his blindness to the great opportunity in 1940 after the defeat of France. One could attribute this outlook to Hitler's Austrian origin, far from the ocean; or believe that he learnt it from some geopolitician in Munich. But essentially it reflected the circumstances of the time. Germany had been defeated by the Western Powers in November 1918; and had herself defeated Russia the preceding January. Hitler, like Stresemann, did not challenge the Western settlement. He did not wish to destroy the British Empire, nor even to deprive the French of Alsace and Lorraine. In return, he wanted the Allies to accept the verdict of January 1918; to abandon the artificial undoing of this verdict after November 1918; and to acknowledge that Germany had been victorious in the East. This was not a preposterous programme. Many Englishmen, to say nothing of Milner and Smuts, agreed with it even in 1918; many more did so later; and most Frenchmen were coming round to the same outlook. The national states of Eastern Europe enjoyed little popularity; Soviet Russia still less. When Hitler aspired to restore the settlement of Brest-Litovsk, he could pose also as the champion of European civilisation against Bolshevism and the Red peril. Maybe his ambitions were genuinely limited to the East; maybe conquest there would have been only the preliminary to conquest in Western Europe or on a World scale. No one can tell. Only events could have given the answer; and by a strange twist of circumstances they never did. Against all expectations, Hitler found himself at war with the Western Powers before he had conquered the East. Nevertheless, Eastern expansion was the primary purpose of his policy, if not the only one. . . .

In principle and doctrine, Hitler was no more wicked and unscrupulous than many other contemporary statesmen. In wicked acts he outdid them all. The policy of Western statesmen also rested ultimately on force—French policy on the army, British policy on sea-power. But these statesmen hoped that it would not be necessary to use this force. Hitler intended to use his force, or would at any rate threaten to use it. If Western morality seemed superior, this was largely because it was the morality of the *status quo;* Hitler's was the immorality of revision. There was a curious, though only superficial, contradiction in Hitler between aims and methods. His aim was change, the overthrow of the existing European order; his method was patience. Despite his bluster and violent talk, he was a master in the game of waiting. He never made a frontal attack on a prepared position—at least never until his judgment had been corrupted by easy victories. Like Joshua before the walls of Jericho, he preferred to wait until the forces opposing him had been sapped by their own confusions and themselves forced success upon him. He had already applied this method to gain power in Germany. He did not "seize" power. He waited for it to be thrust upon him by the men who had previously tried to keep him out. In January 1933 Papen and Hindenburg were imploring him to become Chancellor; and he graciously consented. So it was to be in foreign affairs. Hitler did not make precise demands. He announced that he was dissatisfied; and then waited for the concessions to pour into his lap, merely holding out his hand for more. Hitler did not know any foreign countries at first hand. He rarely listened to his foreign minister, and never read the reports of the his ambassadors. He judged foreign statesmen by intuition. He was convinced that he had taken the measure of all *bourgeois* politicians. German and foreign alike, and that their nerve would crumble before his did. . . .

Who first raised the storm and launched the march of events? The accepted answer is clear: it was Hitler. The moment of his doing so is also accepted: it was on 5 November 1937. We have a record of the statements which he made that day. It is called "the Hossbach memorandum," after the man who made it. This record is supposed to reveal Hitler's plans. Much play was made with it at Nuremberg; and the editors of the *Documents on German Foreign Policy* say that "it provides a summary of German foreign policy in 1937–38." It is therefore worth looking at in detail. Perhaps we shall find it in the explanation of the second World war; or perhaps we shall find only the source of a legend.

That afternoon Hitler called a conference at the Chancellery. It was attended by Blomberg, the minister of war; Neurath, the foreign minister; Fritsch, commander-in-chief of the army; Raeder, commander-in-chief of the navy; and Goering, commander-in-chief of the air force. Hitler did most of the talking. He began with a general disquisition on Germany's need for *Lebensraum.* He did not specify where this was to be found—probably in Europe, though he also discussed colonial gains. But gains there must be. "Germany had to reckon with two hate-inspired antagonists, Britain and France. . . . Germany's problem could only be solved by means of force and this was never without attendant risk." When and how was there to be this resort to force? Hitler discussed three "cases." The first "case" was "period 1943–1945." After that the situation could only change for the worse; 1943 must be the moment for action. Case 2 was civil war in France; if that happened, "the time for action against the Czechs had come." Case 3 was war between France and Italy. This might well occur in 1938; then "our objective must be to overthrow Czechoslovakia and Austria simultaneously." None of these "cases" came true; clearly therefore they do not provide the blueprint for German policy. Nor did Hitler dwell on them. He went on to demonstrate that Germany would gain her aims without a great war; "force" apparently meant to him the threat of war, not necessarily war itself. The Western Powers would be too hampered and too timid to intervene. "Britain almost certainly, and probably France as well, had written off the Czechs and were reconciled to the fact that this question of Germany would be cleared up in due course." No other Power would intervene. "Poland—with Russia in her rear —will have little inclination to engage in war against a victorious Germany." Russia would be held in check by Japan.

Hitler's exposition was in large part day-dreaming, unrelated to what followed in real life. Even if seriously meant, it was not a call to action, at any rate not to action of a great war; it was a demonstration that a great war would not be necessary. Despite the preliminary talk about 1943–1945, its solid core

was the examination of the chances for peaceful triumphs in 1938, when France would be preoccupied elsewhere. Hitler's listeners remained doubtful. The generals insisted that the French army would be superior to the German even if engaged against Italy as well. Neurath doubted whether a Mediterranean conflict between France and Italy were imminent. Hitler waved these doubts aside: "he was convinced of Britain's non-participation, and therefore he did not believe in the probability of belligerent action by France against Germany." There is only one safe conclusion to be drawn from this rambling disquisition: Hitler was gambling on some twist of fortune which would present him with success in foreign affairs, just as a miracle had made him Chancellor in 1933. There was here no concrete plan, no directive for German policy in 1937 and 1938. Or if there were a directive, it was to wait upon events.

Why then did Hitler hold this conference? This question was not asked at Nuremberg; it has not been asked by historians. Yet surely it is an elementary part of historical discipline to ask of a document not only what is in it, but why it came into existence. The conference of 5 November 1937 was a curious gathering. Only Goering was a Nazi. The others were old-style Conservatives who had remained in office to keep Hitler under control; all of them except Raeder were to be dismissed from their posts within three months. Hitler knew that all except Goering were his opponents; and he did not trust Goering much. Why did he reveal his inmost thoughts to men whom he distrusted and whom he was shortly to discharge? This question has an easy answer: he did not reveal his inmost thoughts. There was no crisis in foreign policy to provoke a broad discussion or sweeping decisions. The conference was a manoeuvre in domestic affairs. Here a storm was brewing. The financial genius of Schacht had made rearmament and full employment possible; but now Schacht was jibbing at further expansion of the armament programme. Hitler feared Schacht and could not answer his financial arguments. He knew only that they were wrong: the Nazi régime could not relax its momentum. Hitler aimed to isolate Schacht from the other Conservatives; and he had herefore to win them for a programme of increased armaments. His geopolitical exposition had no other purpose. The Hossbach memorandum itself provides evidence of this. Its last paragraph reads: "The second part of the conference was concerned with questions of armament." This, no doubt, was why it had been called. . . .

Hitler, it is claimed, decided on war, and planned it in detail on 5 November 1937. Yet the Hossbach memorandum contains no plans of the kind, and would never have been supposed to do so, unless it had been displayed at Nuremberg. The memorandum tells us, what we knew already, that Hitler (like every other German statesman) intended Germany to become the dominant Power in Europe. It also tells us that he speculated how this might happen. His speculations were mistaken. They bear hardly any relation to the actual outbreak of war in 1939. A racing tipster who only reached Hitler's level of accuracy would not do well for his clients.

The speculations were irrelevant as well as mistaken. Hitler did not make plans—for world conquest or for anything else. He assumed that others would provide opportunities, and that he would seize them. The opportunities

which he envisaged on 5 November 1937 were not provided. Others were. . . .

Anschluss: the End of Austria

The Austrian affair was under weigh. It had not been launched by Hitler. It was sprung on him by surprise, and he took a chance as always. There was here no planned aggression, only hasty improvisation. Papen, not Hitler, started the ball rolling; and he did so for casual motives of personal prestige. No doubt chance provided that he should give the decisive push; yet it was strangely appropriate that the man who had frivolously brought Hitler to power in Germany should also be the one who, with equal frivolity, started Germany's advance towards European domination. . . .

Schuschnigg[1] had intended to appear at Berchtesgaden as the aggrieved party . . . It was Hitler who laid down terms for future co-operation. Schuschnigg was to make Seyss-Inquart, a supposedly respectable nationalist, Minister of the Interior and to give him control of the police. Austria was to coordinate her economic and foreign policy with that of Germany. Schuschnigg raised constitutional objections: he could not make binding promises without the consent of the Austrian government and President. He was bullied by Hitler; German generals, waiting outside, were ostentatiously called in. Yet, though these methods were abominable, Schuschnigg got most of what he wanted. His constitutional scruples were respected: in the final draft he merely "held out the prospect of the following measures." Seyss-Inquart was no worse than other German nationalists already

[1] Kurt von Schuschnigg (1897–) was Chancellor of Austria from 1934 until the Nazi occupation in 1937, at which time he was held in prison and concentration camp. He was liberated in 1945.—*Ed.*

in the Cabinet: and was indeed a boy-hood friend of Schuschnigg—not that this prevented his becoming a Nazi later. Schuschnigg had long acknowledged that Austria was "a German state;" and this had implied a coordination of policy. He received what he believed to be the vital concession: the illegal activities of the Austrian Nazis were repudiated, and it was agreed that any unwanted Austrian Nazis should "transfer their residence to the Reich."

[This] agreement of 12 February [1938] was not the end of Austria; it was a further step in the "evolutionary solution" which Hitler had laid down. Schuschnigg made no attempt to dis-avow it when he had escaped from Hit-ler's presence. On the contrary he duly secured its confirmation by the Austrian government. Hitler, on his side, assumed that the crisis was over. On 12 February he told the attendant generals to keep up "military pressure shamming action" until 15 February. After this not even a show of action was maintained. On 20 February Hitler addressed the Reich-stag. His main concern was to explain away the dismissal of the conservative ministers: but the agreement over Aus-tria of 12 February enabled him to ride off on a more attractive subject. There was no attack on Schuschnigg, as there would surely have been if Hitler were already projecting aggression against Austria. Quite the reverse, Hitler an-nounced in gentle tones: "Friendly co-operation between the two countries in every field has been assured"; and he concluded: "I would like to thank the Austrian Chancellor in my own name, and in that of the German people, for his understanding and kindness." The following day Hitler kept his part of the bargain. Leopold, the leader of the Nazi underground in Austria, was summoned before Hitler; told that his activities had

been "insane"; and ordered to leave Austria along with his principal asso-ciates. A few days later Hitler saw these Nazis again, gave them another rating, and insisted that "the evolutionary course be taken, whether or not the possi-bility of success could today be foreseen. The Protocol signed by Schuschnigg was so far-reaching that if completely carried out the Austrian problem would be au-tomatically solved." Hitler was satisfied. He made no preparations for action but waited impassively for the automatic solution to mature.

Once more, and for the last time [in March 1938], the initiative came from Schuschnigg. In a puzzled, hesitant way, he built up resentment against the treat-ment he had received at Berchtesgaden and against the consequences of his own weakness. He resolved to arrest the in-evitable slide into a National Socialist Austria by a dramatic challenge. . . . he determined to use Hitler's own method of a plebiscite, and to ask the Austrian people whether they wished to remain independent. . . .

Hitler responded as though someone had trodden on a painful corn. He had received no warning, and had made no preparations. It was clear to him that "the evolutionary solution" was dead. He must either act or be humiliated; and he could not accept humiliation when the breach with the conservative ministers was just behind him. The military leaders were hastily summoned to Berlin. The German army was not yet equipped for any kind of serious campaign; but orders were issued that such forces as were stationed near Aus-tria should be ready to cross the frontier on 12 March. . . .

The German army was invading Austria, or rather marching in to the general enthusiasm of the population For what purpose? Seyss-Inquart was

Chancellor. Goering had told Henderson that the troops would be withdrawn "as soon as the situation was stable" and that thereafter "completely free elections would be held without any intimidation whatever." This had been the original Nazi plan, as botched up on 11 March. Seyss-Inquart thought that everything was successfully concluded with his own appointment, and at 2:30 a.m. on 12 March asked that the invasion should be stopped. He was told that this was impossible; and the German troops rolled on, though with some difficulty. The forces were not prepared for action; and 70% of their vehicles broke down on the road from the frontier to Vienna. Hitler, too, entered Austria on the morning of 12 March. At Linz, where he had gone to school, he addressed the excited crowds. He succumbed to this excitement himself. As he went on to the balcony of Linz Town Hall, he made a sudden, unexpected decision: instead of setting up a tame government in Vienna, he would incorporate Austria in the *Reich.* Seyss-Inquart, Chancellor for a day, was told to issue a law, ordering himself and Austria out of existence. He did so on 13 March. The Anschluss was submitted for approval to the people of Greater Germany. On 10 April 99.08% voted in favour, a genuine reflection of German feeling. . . .

The belief soon became established that Hitler's seizure of Austria was a deliberate plot, devised long in advance, and the first steps towards the domination of Europe. This belief was a myth. The crisis of March 1938 was provoked by Schussnigg, not by Hitler. There had been no German preparations, military or diplomatic. Everything was improvised in a couple of days—policy, promises, armed force. Though Hitler certainly meant to establish control over Austria, the way in which this came

about was for him a tiresome accident, an interruption of his long-term policy, not the maturing of carefully thought-out plans. But the effects could not be undone. There was the effect on Hitler himself. He had got away with murder—the murder of an independent state, even though its independence was largely sham. Hitler's self-confidence was increased, and with it his contempt for the statesmen of other countries. He became more impatient and careless, readier to speed up negotiations by threats of force. In return, statesmen elsewhere began to doubt Hitler's good faith. Even those who still hoped to appease him began to think also of resistance. The uneasy balance tilted, though only slightly, away from peace and towards war. Hitler's aims might still appear justifiable; his methods were condemned. By the Anschluss—or rather by the way in which it was accomplished —Hitler took the first step in the policy which was to brand him as the greatest of war criminals. Yet he took this step unintentionally. Indeed he did not know that he had taken it. . . .

Hitler and Czechoslovakia

Even more than in the case of Austria, Hitler did not need to act. Others would do his work for him. The crisis over Czechoslovakia was provided for Hitler. He merely took advantage of it. . . .

[On May 20 the Czech government accused Hitler of aggressive intentions, called up reservists, and manned the frontiers. These events had] a dramatic effect on Hitler. He was enraged at his apparent humiliation. Seizing the draft directive of 20 May which Keitel[2] had prepared for him, he struck out the first sentence—which repudiated military ac-

[2] Field Marshal Wilhelm Keitel, then Chief of the High Command of the Army, was hanged as a war criminal in 1946.—*Ed.*

tion against Czechoslovakia—and wrote instead: "It is my unalterable intention to smash Czechoslovakia by military action in the near future." Here seems the decisive proof that Hitler was resolved to attack Czechoslovakia, whatever the circumstances. The proof is less decisive than it seems. Even the document from which the damning sentence is taken goes on to assert, in Hitler's usual way, that France would hesitate to intervene "as a result of Italy's unequivocal attitude on our side." The sentence was in fact a momentary display of temper. Hitler soon reverted to his old line. A General Strategical Directive of 18 June stated: "I shall only decide to take action against Czechoslovakia if, as in the case of the occupation of the demilitarised zone and the entry into Austria, I am firmly convinced that France will not march and therefore Britain will not intervene either." Of course Hitler knew that his generals feared war with France, and may have planned to involve them in this war against their will. He played a game of bluff with everyone—with the Western Powers, with the generals, even with himself. There are solid grounds for believing that it was bluff. Few preparations were made for even a defensive war against France. . . .

The conference at Munich was meant to mark the beginning of an epoch in European affairs. "Versailles"—the system of 1919—was not only dead, but buried. A new system, based on equality and mutual confidence between the four great European Powers, was to take its place. Chamberlain said: "I believe that it is peace for our time"; Hitler declared: "I have no more territorial demands to make in Europe". . . . Yet, within six months, a new system was being constructed against Germany. Within a year, Great Britain, France, and Germany were at war. Was "Munich" a fraud from the start—for Germany merely a stage in the march towards world conquest, or, on the side of Great Britain and France, merely a device to buy time until their re-armament was more advanced? So it appeared in retrospect. When the policy of Munich failed, everyone announced that he had expected it to fail; and the participants not only accused the others of cheating, but boasted that they had been cheating themselves. In fact, no one was as clearsighted as he later claimed to have been; and the four men of Munich were all in their different ways sincere, though each had reserves which he concealed from the others. . . .

British policy over Czechoslovakia originated in the belief that Germany had a moral right to the Sudeten German territory, on grounds of national principle; and it drew the further corollary that this victory for self-determination would provide a stabler, more permanent peace in Europe. The British government were not driven to acknowledge the dismemberment of Czechoslovakia solely from fear of war. They deliberately set out to impose this cession of territory on the Czechs before the threat of war raised its head. The settlement at Munich was a triumph for British policy, which had worked precisely to this end; not a triumph for Hitler, who had started with no such clear intention. Nor was it merely a triumph for selfish or cynical British statesmen, indifferent to the fate of far-off peoples or calculating that Hitler might be launched into war against Soviet Russia. It was a triumph for all that was best and most enlightened in British life; a triumph for those who had preached equal justice between peoples; a triumph for those who had courageously denounced the harshness and short-sightedness of Versailles. . . . With skill and persistence, Chamberlain brought first the French, and then the Czechs, to follow the moral line. . . .

[After the Munich Agreement] everyone talked of Hitler's next move in one direction or another. The man who talked, and apparently thought, of it least was Hitler himself. The precise timetable attributed to him by many writers—Munich in September 1938, Prague in March 1939, Danzig in September rests on no contemporary evidence. After his dazzling success at Munich, Hitler returned to the Berghof, where he spent his time drawing dreamplans for the rebuilding of Linz, the Austrian town where he went to school. Occasionally he grumbled at being denied a war against Czechoslovakia. But men must be judged by what they do, not by what they say afterwards. Once more he waited for events to provide him with future success. The military leaders sought a directive for their next activities. Hitler replied on 21 October: "The Wehrmacht must at all times be prepared for the following: (i) securing the frontiers of the German Reich and protection against surprise air attacks, (ii) liquidation of the remainder of the Czech state." These were measures of precaution, not plans for aggression. The continuation of the directive makes this clear: "It must be possible to smash the remainder of the Czech state, should it pursue an anti-German policy." On 17 December the Wehrmacht was told: "Outwardly it must be quite clear that it is only a peaceful action and not a warlike undertaking." These directives have often been quoted as proof that Hitler was never sincere in accepting the Munich settlement. The truth is rather that Hitler doubted whether the settlement would work. Though often regarded as politically ignorant, he un-

derstood better than other European statesmen the problem of Bohemia; and believed, without sinister intention, that independent Czechoslovakia could not survive, when deprived of her natural frontiers and with Czech prestige broken. This was not a wish for Czechoslovakia's destruction. . . .

[In March 1939] Germany hastily recognised Slovak independence, and therewith brought Czecho-Slovakia to an end. What was to happen to the Czech remnant? There was no one to guide it. Beneš had resigned and left the country immediately after Munich. Hacha, his successor, was an elderly lawyer of no political experience. Bewildered, helpless, he could only turn to the great German dictator. Like Schuschnigg before him, he asked to be received by Hitler; and his request was granted. In Berlin he was received with the honours due to a head of state; and then instructed to sign away the independence of his country. Any fragment of reluctance was silenced by the threat that, otherwise, Prague would immediately be bombed. This was the most casual of Hitler's many improvisations. As he confessed later, the German airfields were shrouded in fog, and no aeroplanes could have left the ground. Hacha hardly needed inducement. He signed as required; and harboured so little resentment that he served as a faithful German subordinate until the end of the war. On 15 March Bohemia became a German protectorate. German troops occupied the country. Hitler spent the night of 15 March in Prague—his only recorded visit. All the world saw in this the culmination of a long-planned campaign. In fact, it was the unforeseen byproduct of developments in Slovakia; and Hitler was acting against the Hungarians rather than against the Czechs. . . . Hitler took the decisive step in his career when he occupied Prague. He did it without design; it brought him slight advantage. He acted only when events had already destroyed the settlement of Munich. But everyone outside Germany, and especially the other makers of that settlement, believed that he had deliberately destroyed it himself. . . .

There followed an underground explosion of public opinion such as the historian cannot trace in precise terms. The occupation of Prague did not represent anything new in Hitler's policy or behaviour. President Hacha had succumbed more easily and more willingly than either Schuschnigg or Beneš. Yet British opinion was stirred as it had not been by the absorption of Austria or the capitulation at Munich. Hitler was supposed to have overstepped the bounds. His word could never be trusted again. Perhaps the exaggerated expectations after Munich produced this reaction. Men had assumed, against all the evidence, that "Peace for our time" meant that there would be no more changes in Europe. Perhaps there was a belief, again unfounded, that British armaments were now more adequate. Again, Conservatives were troubled by the "embarrassing" matter of the guarantee, which they had supposed really ment something. In a way impossible to define, those who had given warnings against Hitler were now listened to, where they had been ignored before. The prophets of woe operated from the most varied premises. Some, like Churchill and the anti-German members of the foreign office, regarded Hitler as merely the latest spokesman for Prussian militarism. Others attributed to him new and more grandiose plans which they claimed to have discovered by reading *Mein Kampf* in the original (Hitler forbade its publication in English). . . .

Hitler and Poland

Hitler's objective was alliance with Poland, not her destruction. Danzig was a tiresome preliminary to be got out of the way. As before, Beck[3] kept it in the way. So long as Danzig stood between Poland and Germany, he could evade the embarrassing offer of a German alliance, and so, as he thought, preserve Polish independence.

Beck's calculations worked, though not precisely as he intended. On 26 March, Lipski[4] returned to Berlin. He brought with him a firm refusal to yield over Danzig, though not a refusal to negotiate. Until this moment everything had gone on in secret, with no public hint of German-Polish estrangement. Now it blazed into the open. Beck, to show his resolve, called up Polish reservists. Hitler, to ease things along as he supposed, allowed the German press to write, for the first time, about the German minority in Poland. There were rumours of German troop movements toward the Polish frontier, just as there had been similar rumours of German movements against Czechoslovakia on 21 May 1938. These new rumours were equally without foundation. They seem to have been started by the Poles . . . The British were ready to believe anything. They did not give a thought to Danzig. They supposed that Poland herself was in imminent danger, and likely to succumb . . .

On 30 March Chamberlain drafted with his own hand an assurance to the Polish government:

If . . . any action were taken which clearly threatened their independence, and which the Polish Government accordingly

[3] Colonel Jósef Beck, Poland's Foreign Minister.—*Ed.*
[4] Josef Lipski, Polish Ambassador to Germany. —*Ed.*

felt obliged to resist with their national forces, His Majesty's Government and the French Government would at once lend them all the support in their power.

That afternoon Beck was discussing with the British ambassador how to implement his proposal of a week earlier for a general declaration, when a telegram from London was brought in. The ambassador read out Chamberlain's assurance. Beck accepted it "between two flicks of the ash off his cigarette.' Two flicks; and British grenadiers would die for Danzig. Two flicks; and the illusory great Poland, created in 1919, signed her death-warrant. The assurance was unconditional: the Poles alone were to judge whether it should be called upon. . . .

The Anglo-Polish alliance was a revolutionary event in international affairs. The British had entered into their first peacetime commitment to a continental Power only three years before, when they made their alliance with France. Then they had stressed that it must be unique, and strictly limited to a defensive purpose in Western Europe. Now they plunged into alliance with a country far in Eastern Europe, and one which, until almost the day before, had been judged not worth the bones of a British grenadier. . . . in taking a stand over Danzig they were on peculiarly weak ground. Danzig was the most justified of German grievances: a city of exclusively German population which manifestly wished to return to the Reich and which Hitler himself restrained only with difficulty. The solution, too, seemed peculiarly easy. Halifax never wearied of suggesting that Danzig should return to German sovereignty, with safeguards for Polish trade.

Hitler wanted this also. The destruc-tion of Poland had been no part of his original project. On the contrary, he had wished to solve the question of Danzig so that Germany and Poland could remain on good terms. . . . Many however believe that Hitler was a modern Attila, loving destruction for its own sake and therefore bent on war without thought of policy. There is no arguing with such dogmas. Hitler was an extraordinary man; and they may well be true. But his policy is capable of rational explanation; and it is on these that history is built. The escape into irrationality is no doubt easier. The blame for war can be put on Hitler's Nihilism instead of on the faults and failures of European statesmen—faults and failures which their public shared. Human blunders, however, usually do more to shape history than human wickedness. At any rate, this is a rival dogma which is worth developing, if only as an academic exercise. Of course Hitler's nature and habits played their part. It was easy for him to threaten, and hard for him to conciliate. This is far from saying that he foresaw, or deliberately projected, the European dominance which he seemed to have achieved by 1942. All statesmen aim to win. The size of the winnings often surprises them.

Rational causes have been found for a deliberate German drive to war in 1939. One is economic; another dogma, this time of crudely Marxist kind. Industrial recovery, it is suggested, was presenting Germany with a crisis of over-production. Faced with the tariff walls of other Powers, she had to conquer new markets or burst at the seams. There is little evidence for this dogma. Germany's problem was credit inflation, not over-production, as Schacht had warned when he resigned in 1938. There was too much government paper and not enough productive power to absorb it. Production was being flogged on, not choking with its own excess. When war came, Germany's conquests—far from providing markets—were greedily exploited for the war-machine. Every satellite country except Hungary had a large credit-balance in Berlin at the end of the war—the Germans, that is, had taken much and exported little. Even so, German armament production was cut back in 1940 and again in 1941; the strain was too great. Hence the economic argument ran against war, not in its favour. Or, at best, the argument was self-consuming. Germany needed the prizes of war, solely in order to make war more successfully.

German armaments in themselves provide a second possible reason why Germany should drive to war. Germany had established a lead in armaments over the other Powers; and this lead would gradually waste away. Hitler himself used this argument, but only in the summer of 1939 when already committed to war; and it was not much more serious than his other argument that he wanted to get the war over in order to devote himself to artistic creation. Previously he had asserted, with more truth, that German preponderance would be at its greatest between 1943 and 1945; and, like all such figures, these really meant "this year, next year, sometime, . . ." The German generals best qualified to judge, argued steadily against war in 1939 on technical grounds; and the better qualified, the firmer their opposition. Hitler did not deny their case; he rejected it as irrelevant. He was intending to succeed without war, or at any rate only with a war so nominal as hardly to be distinguished from diplomacy. He was not projecting a major war; hence it did not matter that Germany was not equipped for one. Hitler deliberately ruled out the "rearmament in depth" which was pressed on him by his technical advisers. He was not interested in preparing for a long war against the Great Powers. He chose instead "rearmament in width"—a front-line army without reserves, adequate only for a quick strike. Under Hitler's direction, Germany was equipped to win the war of nerves—the only war he understood and liked; she was not equipped to conquer Europe. Great Britain and France were already secure from a strictly defensive point of view. As the years passed, they would become more so. But Germany's advantage for the immediate blow would remain. Nothing would be lost by the passage of time; and diplomatically much might be gained. In considering German armament we escape from the mystic regions of Hitler's psychology and find an answer in the realm of fact. The answer is clear. The state of German armament in 1939 gives the decisive proof that Hitler was not contemplating general war, and probably not intending war at all.

. . . The old, simple explanation reasserts itself. The war of 1939, far from being premeditated, was a mistake, the result on both sides of diplomatic blunders. . . .

The crisis of August 1939 which led to the Second World War was, ostensibly at any rate, a dispute over Danzig. This dispute was formulated in the last days of March, when Germany made demands concerning Danzig and the Corridor, and the Poles rejected them. From that moment everyone expected Danzig to be the next great topic of international conflict. Yet, in strange contrast to earlier crises, there were no negotiations over Danzig, no attempts to discover a solution; not even attempts to screw up the tension. This paradoxical calm was partly caused by the local situation at

Danzig. Here both Germany and Poland had an impregnable position so long as they did not move; a step by either would start the avalanche. Hence there could be none of the manoeuvres and bargaining which had marked the Czechoslovak crisis. The Sudeten Nazis, like the Austrians before them, built up the tension gradually without guidance from Hitler. In Danzig the tension was already complete; and Hitler, so far as he did anything, held the local Nazis back. . . .

After 26 March Hitler did not again formulate demands concerning Danzig until the day before war broke out. This was not surprising; it was his usual method. So he had waited for offers from Schuschnigg over Austria; so he had waited for offers from Beneš, from Chamberlain, finally from the conference at Munich over Czechoslovakia. Then he did not wait in vain. Did he appreciate that this time no offer would come from the Poles? It seems so from the record. On 3 April he issued instructions that preparations for an attack on Poland "must be made in such a way that the operation can be carried out at any time as from 1 September 1939." But a further directive a week later explained that these preparations were purely precautionary, "should Poland change her policy . . . and adopt a threatening attitude towards Germany." On 23 May, however, he spoke with less reserve to a gathering of generals: "There will be war. Our task is to isolate Poland. . . . It must not come to a simultaneous showdown with the West." This sounds clear enough. But Hitler's real plans are not so easily detected. He had talked just as bravely about war against Czechoslovakia in 1938; yet then, almost certainly, he was playing for victory in the war of nerves. Now, too, preparations had to be made

for war whether he were planning to win by war or diplomacy. When Hitler talked to his generals, he talked for effect, not to reveal the workings of his mind. He knew that the generals disliked and distrusted him; he knew that some of them had planned to overthrow him in September 1938; probably he knew that they were constantly sounding the alarm at the British and French embassies. He wanted to impress the generals and, at the same time, to frighten them. Hence on 23 May he talked not only of war against Poland, which he may have seriously intended; but even of a great war against the Western Powers, which was undoubtedly not part of his plan. Hitler's calculation worked: no sooner was the conference of 23 May ended than the generals, from Goering downwards, were imploring the Western Powers to bring Poland to reason while there was still time. . . .

Nazi Soviet Pact and World War II

It was no doubt disgraceful that Soviet Russia should make any agreement with the leading Fascist state; but this reproach came ill from the statesmen who went to Munich and who were then sustained in their own countries by great majorities. . . . Both Hitler and Stalin imagined that they had prevented war, not brought it on. Hitler thought that he would score another Munich over Poland; Stalin that he had at any rate escaped an unequal war in the present, and perhaps even avoided it altogether. . . .

At any rate the bomb had exploded. Hitler was radiant, confident that he had pulled off the decisive stroke. On 22 August he entertained his leading generals to the wildest of his speeches: "Close your hearts to pity. Act brutally." This rigmarole was not a serious directive for action—no formal record was kept. Hitler was glorying in his own skill. Tucked away in the speech was a hard core: "Now the probability is great that the West will not intervene." As well, Hitler was talking for effect. A report of the speech reached the British embassy almost at once; whether intentionally or not, the so-called German "resistance" did Hitler's work for him. On 23 August Hitler took a further step. He fixed the attack on Poland for 4:40 a.m. on 26 August. This, too, was play-acting to impress the generals and, through them, the Western Powers. The German time-table could operate only from 1 September. Before then an attack on Poland was possible only if she had already surrendered. But technical considerations no longer seemed to matter: the Nazi-Soviet pact was assumed to have cleared the way for a diplomatic collapse on the part of the Western Powers. . . .

On 23 August Sir Horace Wilson, acting on Chamberlain's behalf, saw Kennedy, the American ambassador. After the conversation, Kennedy telephoned the State Department: "The British wanted one thing of us and one thing only, namely that we put pressure on the Poles. They felt that they could not, given their obligations, do anything of this sort but that we could." President Roosevelt rejected this idea out of hand. Chamberlain—again according to Kennedy—then lost all hope: "He says the futility of it all is the thing that is frightful; after all, they cannot save the Poles; they can merely carry on a war of revenge that will mean the destruction of all Europe."

The deadlock lasted until 29 August. Then it was broken by Hitler. He was in the weaker position, though the British did not know it. There was not much time left before 1 September for him to pull off diplomatic success. At 7:15 p.m.

he made to Henderson[5] a formal offer and a formal demand: he would negotiate directly with Poland if a Polish plenipotentiary arrived in Berlin the following day. . . . But the decision rested with the British government. Here was the proposal which they had always wanted and which they had repeatedly hinted at to Hitler: direct negotiations between Poland and Germany. Hitler had now done his part; but they could not do theirs. They had the gravest doubt whether the Poles would thus present themselves in Berlin at Hitler's behest. Kennedy reported Chamberlain's feeling to Washington: "Frankly, he is more worried about getting the Poles to be reasonable than the Germans." The British gnawed over the problem throughout 30 August. Finally they hit on a sort of solution. They passed Hitler's demand on to Warsaw at 12:25 a.m. on 31 August—that is to say, twenty-five minutes after the German ultimatum, if such it were, had expired. The British had been correct in their apprehension of Polish obstinacy. Beck, when informed of Hitler's demand, at once replied: "if invited to Berlin he would of course not go, as he had no intention of being treated like President Hacha." Thus the British, by acting too late, could still claim that they had offered something which they knew they could not deliver: a Polish plenipotentiary in Berlin.

Hitler had not anticipated this. He had expected that negotiations would start; and he then intended them to break down on Polish obstinacy. On his instructions detailed demands were at last prepared. These were principally the immediate return of Danzig, and a plebiscite in the Corridor—the very terms

[5] Sir Nevile Meyrick Henderson, British ambassador to Germany, 1937–1939.—*Ed.*

which the British and French governments had themselves long favoured. But, failing a Polish plenipotentiary, the Germans had difficulty in making their terms known. At midnight on 30 August Henderson brought to Ribbentrop the news that a Polish plenipotentiary was not coming that day. Ribbentrop had only the rough draft of the proposed German terms, scribbled over with Hitler's emendations. It was not in a condition to be shown to Henderson; and Ribbentrop had instructions from Hitler not to do so. He therefore read the terms over slowly. Later a myth grew up that he had "gabbled" them, deliberately cheating Henderson with terms that were only for show. In fact Henderson got the gist clearly, and was impressed. Taken at their face value, he thought, they were "not unreasonable." On his return to the British embassy, he summoned Lipski at 2 a.m., and urged him to seek an interview with Ribbentrop at once. Lipski took no notice, and went back to bed. . . .

At 12:40 p.m. on 31 August Hitler decided that the attack should proceed. At 1 p.m. Lipski telephoned, asking for an interview with Ribbentrop. The Germans, who had intercepted his instructions, knew that he had been told not to enter into "any concrete negotiations." At 3 p.m. Weizsäcker[6] telephoned Lipski to ask whether he was coming as a plenipotentiary. Lipski replied: "No, in his capacity as an ambassador." This was enough for Hitler. The Poles, it seemed, were remaining obstinate; he could go forward to the gamble of isolating them in war. At 4 p.m. the orders for war were confirmed. At 6:30 p.m. Lipski at last saw Ribbentrop. Lipski said that his government were "favourably considering" the British proposal for direct Polish-German negotiations. Ribbentrop asked whether he was a plenipotentiary. Lipski again answered No. Ribbentrop did not communicate the German terms; if he had tried to do so, Lipski would have refused to receive them. Thus ended the only direct contact between Germany and Poland since 26 March. The Poles had kept their nerve unbroken to the last moment. At 4:45 a.m. on the following morning the German attack on Poland began. At 6 a.m. German aeroplanes bombed Warsaw. . . .

The British ultimatum was delivered to the Germans at 9 a.m. on 3 September. It expired at 11 a.m., and a state of war followed. When Bonnet[7] learnt that the British were going to war in any case, his overriding anxiety was to catch up with them. The time of the French ultimatum was advanced, despite the supposed objections of the General Staff: it was delivered at noon on 3 September and expired at 5 p.m. In this curious way the French who had preached resistance to Germany for twenty years appeared to be dragged into war by the British who had for twenty years preached conciliation. Both countries went to war for that part of the peace settlement which they had long regarded as least defensible. Hitler may have projected a great war all along; yet it seems from the record that he became involved in war through launching on 29 August a diplomatic manoeuvre which he ought to have launched on 28 August.

Such were the origins of the second World war. . . .

---

[6] Baron Ernst von Weizsäcker, State Secretary in the German Foreign Office.—*Ed.*

[7] Georges Bonnet, French Minister of Foreign Affairs, 1938–1939.—*Ed.*

H. R. TREVOR-ROPER (1914–   ) earned his
spurs as a historian with his studies of seventeenth-
century England and his biography of Archbishop
Laud. His professional interest in the Nazi period
began when as an officer in the British Intelligence
Bureau during World War II he was commissioned
to find out whether Hitler had actually committed
suicide. His inquiries led to the brilliant book,
The Last Days of Hitler (London and New York,
1947). In this review essay the acerbic Oxford
historian engages in one of his favorite indoor
sports: intellectual jousting with his professional
rival, A. J. P. Taylor. What reasons are there
for supporting one antagonist against the other?
Which interpretation of Hitler and Nazi Germany
seems more consistent with the evidence?*

Taylor's Views Disputed

The thesis is perfectly clear. According to Mr. Taylor, Hitler was an ordinary German statesman in the tradition of Stresemann and Brüning, differing from them not in methods (he was made Chancellor for "solidly democratic reasons") nor in ideas (he had no ideas) but only in the greater patience and stronger nerves with which he took advantage of the objective situation in Europe. His policy, in so far as he had a policy, was no different from that of his predecessors. He sought neither war nor annexation of territory. He merely sought to restore Germany's "natural" position in Europe, which had been artificially altered by the Treaty of Versailles: a treaty which, for that reason, "lacked moral validity from the start." Such a restoration might involve the recovery of lost German territory like Danzig, but it did not entail the direct government even of Austria or the Sudetenland, let alone Bohemia. Ideally, all that Hitler required was that Austria, Czechoslovakia, and other small Central European states, while remaining independent, should become political satellites of Germany.

Of course it did not work out thus, But that, we are assured, was not Hitler's fault. For Hitler, according to Mr. Taylor, never took the intiative in politics. He "did not make plans—for world-conquest or anything else. He assumed that others would provide opportunities

* Reprinted from H. R. Trevor-Roper, "A. J. P. Taylor, Hitler and the War" in *Encounter*, vol. XVII (July, 1961). Copyright © 1961 by H. R. Trevor-Roper. Reprinted by permission of A. D. Peters & Co. and Harold Matson Co.

and that he would seize them." And that is what happened. The Austrian crisis of March 1938, we are told, "was provoked by Schuschnigg, not by Hitler." Hitler was positively embarrassed by it: "he was Austrian enough to find the complete disappearance of Austria inconceivable until it happened." Similarly we learn that the Sudeten crisis of 1938 was created by the Sudeten Nazis, who "built up the tension gradually, without guidance from Hitler": Hitler himself "merely took advantage of it." Having taken advantage of it at Munich, he had no intention of going on and annexing the Czech lands: "he merely doubted whether the settlement would work . . . [he] believed, without sinister intention, that independent Czechoslovakia could not survive when deprived of her natural frontiers and with Czech prestige broken." So, within six months, as "the unforeseen by-product of developments in Slovakia," he felt obliged to tear up the settlement and occupy Prague; but there was "nothing sinister or premeditated" in that. It was an unfortunate necessity forced upon him by the unskilful President Hacha. The Polish crisis of 1939 was similarly forced upon him by Beck. "The destruction of Poland," we are told, "had been no part of his original project. On the contrary, he wished to solve the question of Danzig so that Germany and Poland could remain on good terms." The last thing he wanted was war. The war of nerves was "the only war he understood and liked." Germany "was not equipped to conquer Europe."

The state of German rearmament in 1939 gives the decisive proof that Hitler was not contemplating general war, and probably not contemplating war at all.

Even on August 23rd, 1939, when the Nazi-Soviet Pact was signed, "both Hitler and Stalin imagined that they had prevented war, not brought it on." What rational person could have supposed that this pact, instead of discouraging the British, would determine them to stand by their commitments? The war, "far from being premeditated, was a mistake, the result on both sides of diplomatic blunders."

Hitler's own share of these diplomatic blunders was, it seems, very small. He "became involved in war," we are told, "through launching on August 29th a diplomatic manoeuvre which he ought to have launched on August 28th." The blunders of the Western statesmen were far more fundamental. For what ought the Western statesmen to have done when faced by Hitler's modest demands? According to Mr. Taylor, they should have conceded them all. . . . Hitler was a statesman who merely sought to reassert Germany's "natural weight," and they would therefore have gained respect by recognising him. Accordingly Mr. Taylor's heroes among Western statesmen are those who recognised German claims: Ramsay MacDonald and Neville Chamberlain. Winston Churchill believed in the balance of power and would have maintained frontiers designed on principles of security, not nationality. Intolerable cynicism! How much nobler was that "triumph for British policy," the Munich settlement! . . .

Munich, according to Mr. Taylor, "atoned" for all the previous weakness of British policy; it was a victory for "morality" (which is his word for political realism) ; and he praises Chamberlain's "skill and persistence" in bringing "first the French and then the Czechs to follow the moral line." If only Chamberlain had not lost his nerve in 1939! If only he had shown equal "skill and persistence" in enabling Hitler to detach Danzig and the Polish Corridor, how happy we should all be! Germany would have recovered its "natural" position, "morality" would have triumphed, and everyone would be happy in the best of possible worlds.

Such, in brief, is Mr. Taylor's thesis. It is not surprising that it has been hailed with cries of delight in neo-Nazi or semi-Nazi circles in Germany. It is more surprising that the book has been greeted by the fashionable Grub Street of England as the highest achievement of British historiography. Mr. Taylor has been compared with Gibbon and Macaulay; his failure to secure worthy promotion has caused astonishment. The anonymous oracle of the *Times Literary Supplement* has predicted finality for the result of his "methodical and impeccable logic." In the *Observer,* Mr. Sebastian Haffner (who recently published a panegyric of that "greatest Roman of them all," Dr. Goebbels) has declared the book "an almost faultless masterpiece" in which "fairness reigns supreme"; and his cosy, middle-brow colleagues in rival papers, hypnotised by a reputation which they are unqualified to test, have obediently jollied their readers along in harmony with the blurb. However, let us not all be hypnotised. Before hurling ourselves down the Gadarene slope, let us ask of Mr. Taylor's thesis, not, Is it brilliant? Is it plausible? but, Is it true? By what rules of evidence, by what philosophy of interpretation is it reached?

Perhaps we may begin by noting Mr. Taylor's general philosophy. Mr. Taylor, it seems, does not believe that human agents matter much in history. His story is "a story without heroes, and perhaps even without villains." "In my opinion," he explains, "statesmen are too absorbed by events to follow a preconceived plan. They take one step and the next follows from it." If they achieve anything, it is by accident not design: "all statesmen aim to win: the size of their winnings often surprises them." The real determinants of history, according to Mr. Taylor, are objective situations and human blunders. . . .

But is this general philosophy true? Do statesmen really never make history? Are they, all of them, always "too absorbed by events to follow a preconceived plan"? Was this true of Richelieu, of Bismarck, of Lenin? In particular, was it true of Hitler? Was Hitler really just a more violent Mr. Micawber sitting in Berlin or Berchtesgaden and waiting for something to turn up: something which, thanks to historic necessity, he could then turn to advantage? Certainly Hitler himself did not think so. He regarded himself as a thinker, a practical philosopher, the demiurge of a new age of history. And since he published a blueprint of the policy which he intended to carry out, ought we not at least to look at this blueprint just in case it had some relevance to his policy? After all, the reason why the majority of the British people reluctantly changed, between 1936 and 1939, from the views of Neville Chamberlain and Mr. Taylor to the views of Winston Churchill was their growing conviction that Hitler meant what he said: that he was aiming —*so oder so,*[1] as he used to say—at world-conquest. A contemporary conviction that was strong enough to change the mood of a nation from a passionate desire for peace to a resolute determination on war surely deserves some respect from the historian. A historian who totally ignores it because, twenty years later, he can interpret some of the documents in an opposite sense runs the risk of being considered too clever by half.

Let us consider briefly the programme

1 "This way or that."—*Ed.*

which Hitler laid down for himself. It was a programme of Eastern colonisation, entailing a war of conquest against Russia. If it were successfully carried out, it would leave Germany dominant in Eurasia and able to conquer the West at will. In order to carry it out, Hitler needed a restored German army which, since it must be powerful enough to conquer Russia, must also be powerful enough to conquer the West if that should be necessary. And that might be necessary even before the attack on Russia. For in order to reach Russia, Hitler would need to send his armies through Poland; and in order to do this—whether by the conquest of Poland or in alliance with it—he would need to break the bonds of treaty and interest which bound the new countries of Eastern Europe, the creatures of Versailles, to their creators, Britain and France. Hitler might be able to break those bonds without war against the West, but he could not be sure of it: it was always possible that a war with the West would be necessary before he could march against Russia. And in fact this is what happened.

Now this programme, which Hitler ascribed to himself, and which he actually carried out, is obviously entirely different from the far more limited programme which is ascribed to him by Mr. Taylor, and which he did not carry out. How then does Mr. Taylor deal with the evidence about it? He deals with it quite simply, either by ignoring it or by denying it as inconsistent with his own theories about statesmen in general and Hitler in particular: theories (one must add) for which he produces no evidence at all.

Take the inconvenient fact of Hitler's avowed programme of a great Eastern land-empire. In spite of some casual admission, Mr. Taylor effectively denies that Hitler had any such programme.

Hitler, he says, "was always the man of daring improvisations: he made lightning decisions and then presented them as the result of long-term policy." Hitler's *Table Talk,* he says airily (as if this were the only evidence for such a programme), "was delivered far in occupied territory during the campaign against Soviet Russia, and *then* Hitler dreamed of some fantastic empire which would rationalize his career of conquest." [My italics here, and in all quotations below]. But why does Mr. Tayor believe, or rather pretend, that it was only in 1942, after his Russian conquests, that Hitler dreamed of an Eastern Empire? His programme had been stated, as clearly as possible, in 1924, in *Mein Kampf,* and on numerous other occasions since. Mr. Taylor hardly ever refers to *Mein Kampf* and never to the other occasions. In 1939, he admits, some people "attributed to Hitler "grandiose plans which *they claimed* to have discovered by reading *Mein Kampf* in the original (Hitler forbade its publication in English)." The implication is that such plans are not to be found in *Mein Kampf* and that those who "claim to have discovered" them had not really read, or been able to read an untranslated work. But the fact is that those plans are unmistakably stated in *Mein Kampf* and that all the evidence of the 1930's showed that Hitler still intended to carry them out. I may add (since Mr. Taylor includes me among those who have ascribed to Hitler "preconceived plans" which he never pursued that I myself read *Mein Kampf* in the original in 1938, and that I read it under the impact of Munich and of the remarkable prophecies of Sir Robert Ensor, who had read it and who insisted that Hitler had meant what he said. By absolutely refusing to face this evidence, and contemptuously dismissing those who have faced it, Mr. Taylor contrives to reach the preposterous conclusion that men like Ensor, who correctly forecast Hitler's future programme from the evidence, were really wrong, and that men like Chamberlain, who did not read the evidence and were proved totally wrong by events, were really right. His sole justification of this paradox is that he has accepted as an axiom a characterisation of Hitler as a "traditional" statesman pursuing limited aims. Mr. Taylor's Hitler cannot have held such views, and therefore the inconvenient fact that the real Hitler uttered such views with remarkable consistency for twenty years and actually put them into practice, is simply puffed aside. When Hitler, in 1941, finally launched that conquest of Russia which, as he himself said, was "the be-all and end-all of Nazism," Mr. Taylor easily explains it away. "By 1941," he says, "Hitler had lost his old gift of patience": he "gratuitously" deviated from his former course; and at the mere thought of such an unaccountable fall from grace, Mr. Taylor promptly ends his book.

Nor is this the only perversion of evidence to which Mr. Taylor has to resort, in order to represent Hitler as a "traditional" statesman. The traditional statesmen *did not seek,* as Hitler did, to incorporate the Sudeten Germans in the Reich. Traditional statesmen demanded the frontiers of 1914; but Hitler, again and again, repudiated the frontiers of 1914 as a contemptible ambition. They looked back, at most, to the war-aims of 1914; he repudiated those war-aims. Even the "natural" position of January 1918, after the huge gains of Brest-Litovsk, was insufficient for Hitler. The treaty of Brest-Litovsk gave Germany the Ukraine as a colony of exploitation, a capitalist colony. But Hitler always made it quite clear that he spurned such a colony: he wanted the Ukraine as a colony of settlement. "I should deem it a crime," he said, "if I sacrificed the blood of a quarter of a million men merely for the conquest of natural riches to be exploited in a capitalist way. The goal of the *Ostpolitik* is to open up an area of settlement for a hundred million Germans." All this is pushed aside by Mr. Taylor with the remark,

When Hitler lamented, "If only we had a Ukraine . . ." he seemed to suppose there were no Ukrainians. Did he propose to exploit, or exterminate them? *Apparently he never considered the question.*

As if Hitler had not made his answer perfectly plain! As if he had any scruples about transporting or even exterminating populations! What about the European Jews! But that episode is conveniently forgotten by Mr. Taylor. It does not fit the character of a traditional German statesman who "in principle and doctrine, was no more wicked and unscrupulous than many other contemporary statesmen."

If Mr. Taylor's cardinal assumptions about Hitler's character and purpose are, to say the least, questionable, what are we to say of his use of evidence to illustrate them? Here he states his method with admirable clarity. "It is an elementary part of historical discipline," he says, "to ask of a document not only what is in it but why it came into existence." With this maxim we may agree, only adding that since the contents of a document are objective evidence while its purpose may be a matter of private surmise, we must not rashly subject the former to the latter. . . .

Now let us take a few instances. On November 5th, 1937, Hitler summoned his war-leaders to the Chancellery and made a speech which, he said, in the event of his death was to be regarded as his "last will and testament." That suggests that he was not talking irresponsibly. The official record of this speech is the so-called "Hossbach Memorandum" which was used at Nuremberg as evidence of Hitler's plans for the gradual conquest of Europe. In it Hitler declared that the aim of German policy must be the conquest of *Lebensraum* in Europe, "but we will not copy liberal capitalist policies which rely on exploiting colonies. It is not a case of conquering people but of conquering agriculturally useful space." That seems clear enough. Then Hitler went on to consider the means of making such conquests. "German politics," he said, "must reckon with two hateful enemies, England and France, to whom a strong German colossus in the centre of Europe would be intolerable." Moreover, he admitted, these two hateful enemies would probably, at some stage, resist him by force: "the German question can only be solved by way of force, and this is never without risk." He then proceeded to discuss hypothetical possibilities. Since the hypothetical circumstances did not in fact arise, we need not dwell on them. The essential points are that the risk of European war must be faced by 1943–5, for "after that we can only expect a change for the worse," and that "our *first* aim" must be, at the first convenient opportunity, "to conquer Czechoslovakia and Austria simultaneously." This first conquest he hoped to achieve without war, for "in all probability England and perhaps also France have already silently written off Czechoslovakia." It could and should therefore be attempted as soon as circumtances make it possible in order that the later, more real risk could be faced before 1943–5. But there was to be no doubt about the nature of the conquest. It was not to be (as Mr. Taylor always maintains) the reduction of Aus-

tria and Czechoslovakia to the role of satellites: it was to be, in Hitler's own words, "the annexation of the two states to Germany, militarily and politically." The idea of satellite states in Eastern Europe, Hitler said in a secret speech delivered only a fortnight later, was one of the futile notions of "traditional" German politicians, and he dismissed it as "idiotic" *(wahnsinnig)*. Finally, it is clear that conquered Austria and Czechoslovakia cannot themselves have constituted the *Lebensraum* which was the ultimate objective. Austria and Czechoslovakia were to be stepping-stones, "in all probability" secured without war, towards larger conquests which would entail a greater risk.

Such was Hitler's "testament" of November 1937. Its content is clear and logical and it has been taken seriously by all historians—until Mr Taylor comes along and tells us that we have all been hoodwinked. For was not this document produced at Nuremberg? All documents produced at Nuremberg, he says, are "loaded," and "anyone who relies on them finds it almost impossible to escape from the load with which they are charged." So Mr. Taylor gives us a sample of his method of using such documents. Why, he asks, was the speech made? "The historian," he observes, "must push through the *cloud of phrases*" (so much for Hitler's perfectly clear statements) "to the *realities* beneath." The speech, he notes, was not made to Nazis but to generals and admirals, and its purpose was clearly to demand greater rearmament. With this we can agree. But Mr. Taylor does not stop there. In order to persuade these "conservative" war-leaders of the necessity of further rearmament, Hitler (he says) had to overcome the economic opposition of Dr. Schacht. His speech therefore *"had no other purpose"* than "to isolate Schacht from the other conservatives"; the dates 1943–5 (to which Hitler consistently kept) *"like all such figures, really meant* 'this year, next year, sometime. . . .' "; and the content of a speech which Hitler himself described as his political testament (but Mr. Taylor does not quote that description) is dismissed as "day-dreaming unrelated to what followed in real life." Why Hitler should be expected to speak more "realistically" on military matters to Nazis at a froth-blowers' meeting than to hardheaded war-leaders who would have to organise and carry out his programme is not clear. Presumably it is "an elementary part of historical discipline" to assume that.

A second example of Mr. Taylor's "historical discipline" is provided by his treatment of the crisis leading to the outbreak of war in 1939. By now Austria and Czechoslovakia had been "annexed to Germany, militarily and politically," and Hitler had turned the heat upon Poland. According to Mr. Taylor, Hitler really only wanted the German city of Danzig, but since geography prevented him from obtaining it except by coercion of Poland, he was forced, reluctantly, to apply such coercion and prepare military plans. Of course (according to Mr. Taylor) he did not intend to execute these plans. His military plans were "only intended to reinforce the diplomatic war of nerves." Unfortunately the British Government, misled after Hitler's occupation of Prague into thinking that he aimed at far larger conquests, had imprudently guaranteed Poland and thus threatened Hitler with European war if he sought this next "natural," "moral" aim by any but peaceful means. . . . Britain, quixotically faithful to the "phrases" of the guarantee, and deluded by the idea that Hitler, if given a free hand, would not stop at Danzig, ignored

all the "realities" of the situation and made war, "war for Danzig."

Such is Mr. Taylor's version of the Polish crisis. In defence of it he finds it necessary here, too, to charm away some important documents, and once again it it instructive to watch the exorcist at work. On May 23rd, 1939, Hitler again summoned his war-leaders. He told them, according to Mr. Taylor, who quotes no other words of the document, "there will be war. Our task is to isolate Poland. . . . It must not come to a simultaneous showdown with the West." "This," comments Mr. Taylor, "seems clear enough"; but he then dismisses even this evidence by saying authoritatively that "when Hitler talked to his generals, he talked for effect, not to reveal the workings of his mind." So that is that. Three months later, with the signature of the Nazi-Soviet Pact, Hitler again addressed his generals, and again Mr. Taylor is content to quote only one sentence from the speech: "now the probability is great that the West will not intervene." Apart from that "hard core," the rest of the speech, he says, can be ignored, as Hitler "was talking for effect." After all, by the Nazi-Soviet Pact, Hitler considered that "he had prevented war, not brought it on." So, once again, Hitler's mere "phrases" dissolve on contact with Mr. Taylor's "realities."

But why should we suppose, as an axiom, that Hitler, when briefing his generals on the eve of a possible war, talked only for effect? Why should we not suppose that he intended them to be ready (as they were) for the real future? And why should we altogether overlook some very clear statements which he made to them? For if we look at the full texts of these two speeches, we find that Mr. Taylor has made certain remarkable omissions.

In the first of these two speeches Hitler

began by insisting that the next step towards Germany's goal could not be taken "without the invasion of foreign states or attacks upon foreign property," and that although bloodless victories had been won in the past, "further successes cannot be obtained without the shedding of blood." *"Danzig,"* he went on, in words from which Mr. Taylor has firmly averted his eyes, *"is not the subject of the dispute at all.* It is a question of expanding our living-space in the East." Moreover, he looked clearly forward to the prospect of war with the West. "The Polish problem," he said, "is inseparable from conflict with the West." For all that, "we are left with the decision to attack Poland at the first opportunity. We cannot expect a repetition of the Czech affair." Of course Hitler hoped to avoid a simultaneous conflict with the West, but he did not rely on any such hope: "the *Führer* doubts the possibility of a peaceful settlement with England. We must prepare ourselves for the conflict." The remaining two-thirds of the document deal with the problems of war with Britain, "the driving-force against Germany." All this is totally ignored by Mr. Taylor: it cannot have been the "hard core" of any argument used by *his* Hitler: therefore, he declares, it was mere froth, uttered for "effect."

In the second speech Hitler similarly made clear statements which Mr. Taylor does not quote. For instance, immediately after the "hard core," the single sentence which he does quote, about the probability that the West will be frightened out of intervention by the Nazi-Soviet Pact, come the words, *"we must accept the risk with reckless resolution";* and Hitler then went on to explain how

Germany, thanks to Russian supplies, could withstand a Western blockade. His only fear, he said, was that "at the last moment some *Schweinhund* will make a proposal for mediation"; a proposal, perhaps, which might have fobbed him off Danzig which, as he had admitted, was "not the subject of the dispute at all." No: Hitler was now resolved on war, even if the West did come in.

I shall give a propagandist cause for starting the war: never mind if it be plausible or not. The victor shall not be asked afterwards whether he told the truth or not.

As for the West, "even if war should break out in the West, the destruction of Poland shall be the primary objective." Which indeed was exactly what happened. By last-minute diplomatic maneuvers Hitler naturally sought to detach the West, but when that could not be done, he went ahead, with his eyes open, into a European war which, though larger than he had hoped, he still reckoned on winning.

I have said enough to show why I think Mr. Taylor's book utterly erroneous. In spite of his statements about "historical discipline," he selects, suppresses, and arranges evidence on no principle other than the needs of his thesis; and that thesis, that Hitler was a traditional statesman, of limited aims, merely responding to a given situation, rests on no evidence at all, ignores essential evidence, and is, in my opinion, demonstrably false. This casuistical defence of Hitler's foreign policy will not only do harm by supporting neo-Nazi mythology: it will also do harm, perhaps irreparable harm, to Mr. Taylor's reputation as a serious historian. . . .

Suggestions for Additional Reading

There is now an enormous literature on Hitler and the Third Reich. The books listed below form a highly selective bibliography designed to give students basic reading on significant aspects of the period. Most of the books listed, in turn, contain valuable suggestions for further reading. This bibliography is arranged in paragraphs according to subject matter.

For listings and reviews of current articles and books, the serious student will wish to follow *Vierteljahrshefte für Zeitgeschichte* (Tübingen), *The Journal of Modern History* (Chicago), *The Journal of Central European Affairs* (Boulder, Colo.), *International Affairs* (London), and the publications of the Wiener Library (London), especially its *Bulletin*.

National Socialism must be studied against the broad background of modern German history. The most useful one-volume account from antiquity to the present is John E. Rhodes, *Germany, A History* (New York, 1964). Two distinguished volumes of a projected three-volume study by the major historian, Hajo Holborn, have appeared: *A History of Germany, The Reformation* (New York, 1959) and *A History of Germany, 1648-1840* (New York, 1964). For the subsequent period, see the excellent study, really a series of interpretive essays, by Koppel S. Pinson, *Modern Germany: Its History and Civilization* (New York, 1954). Also on the later period, A. J. P. Taylor's *The Course of German History* (New York, 1946) is always provocative, sometimes brilliant, though occasionally irresponsible. For a provocative comparative study of Fascism, see Ernst Nolte, *Three Faces of Fascism* (New York, 1966); also useful is F. L. Carsten, *The Rise of Fascism* (Berkeley, Calif., 1967).

For the immediate background of the Weimar Republic, William Halperin, *Germany Tried Democracy, A Political History of the Reich from 1918-1933* (New York, 1946; reprinted 1963) is still an excellent survey. A left-wing socialist account may be found in Arthur Rosenberg, *The Birth of the German Republic, 1871-1918* (New York, 1931) and in his less penetrating *A History of the German Republic* (London, 1936). An important work that stresses political history is Erich Eyck, *A History of the Weimar Republic*, 2 vols., translated by Harlan P. Hanson and Robert G. L. Waite (Cambridge, Mass., 1963-64). On the transitional period between Weimar and Hitler, see the magisterial study, Karl Dietrich Bracher, *Die Auflösung der Weimarer Republik*, 3rd ed. (Villingen, Schwarzwald, 1960). An excellent brief treatment of the Weimar Republic and the immediate setting for the advent of Hitler is given in A. J. Nicholls, *Weimar and the Rise of Hitler* (St. Martin's Paperback, New York, 1968). See also the penetrating study in microcosmic history by W. S. Allen, *The Nazi Seizure of Power, The Experience of a Single German Town, 1930-1935* (New York, 1966); and useful essays in *The Path to Dictatorship, 1918-1933, Ten Essays by German Scholars* (Anchor Paperback, New York, 1966).

Noteworthy biographical studies of Weimar leaders include Klaus Epstein, *Matthias Erzberger and the Dilemma of German Democracy* (Princeton, N.J., 1959); Hans W. Gatzke, *Stresemann and the Rearmament of Germany* (Baltimore, Md. 1954); John W. Wheeler-Bennett, *The Wooden Titan, Hindenburg in Twenty Years of German History* (New York, 1936); Andreas Dorpalen, *Hindenburg and the Weimar Republic*

(Princeton, N.J., 1964); and Henry Ashby Turner, Jr., *Stresemann and the Politics of the Weimar Republic* (Princeton, N.J., 1963).

Valuable special studies of the period include: Walter H. Kaufmann, *Monarchism in the Weimar Republic* (New York, 1952); Ossip K. Flechtheim, *Die kommunistische Partei Deutschlands in der Weimarer Republik* (Offenbach-am-Main, 1948); and Werner Angress, *Stillborn Revolution: The Communist Bid for Power in Germany, 1921-23* (Princeton, N.J., 1963.)

The fascinating and difficult · question of the causes of Nazism has been discussed by many writers. A valuable collection of differing German interpretations may be found in Hans Kohn (ed.), *German History: Some New German Views* (Boston, 1954). See also the essays, notably by Baumont, Schokking, Poliakov, Ritter, Lütge, and Taylor, in a collection edited by Maurice Baumont, John H. E. Fried, and Edmond Vermeil, *The Third Reich* (New York, 1955). An excellent bibliographical essay evaluating various interpretations of Hitler's Germany is Andrew G. Whiteside, "The Nature and Origins of National Socialism," *The Journal of Central European Affairs*, vol. XVII, no. 1 (April, 1957), pp. 48-73.

Gerhard Ritter, a prolific and influential German historian, joins others of his countrymen in insisting that the Third Reich was not caused by any alleged "Nazi mentality" in the German people. Rather, it was the consequence of certain pan-European phenomena dating from Rousseau, the French Revolution, and industrialization—tendencies which fostered "democratic radicalism" in the lower classes and invited demagogues to seize power and tyrannize the masses in the name of the people. Ritter's interpretation is presented briefly in an English essay appearing in the previously cited work edited by Baumont *et al.*, *The Third Reich*. A different explanation is given by the major German historian, Friedrich Meinecke; writing in his reflective work, *The German Catastrophe,* translated by Sidney B. Fay (Cambridge, Mass., 1950), Meinecke concludes that National Socialism

succeeded because it subverted and exploited the two dominant tendencies of the modern epoch: nationalism and socialism.

Subtle questions of national character are treated sympathetically by Robert H. Lowie, *Toward Understanding Germany* (1954); while Richard M. Brickner, M.D., *Is Germany Incurable?* (Philadelphia, 1943) argues that the Germans are paranoid. See also David Rodnick, *Postwar Germans, An Anthropologist's Account* (New Haven, Conn., 1948). The various Germanophobe writings of Lord Vansittart, including *Black Record: Germans Past and Present* (London, 1941), have produced a considerable response such as H. N. Brailsford, *Germans and Nazis— A Reply to 'Black Record'* (London, 1944) and Harold J. Laski, *The Germans—Are They Human? A Reply to Sir Robert Vansittart* (London, 1941). See also Louis L. Snyder, *German Nationalism: The Tragedy of a People* (Harrisburg, Pa., 1952) and G. P. Gooch *et al.* (eds.), *The German Mind and Outlook* (London, 1945). Psychological studies of value include Erich Fromm, *Escape from Freedom* (New York, 1941); Zevedei Barbu, *Democracy and Dictatorship: Their Psychology and Patterns of Life* (New York, 1956); Theodore Abel, *Why Hitler Came into Power: An Answer Based on the Original Life Stories of Six Hundred of his Followers* (New York, 1938); T. W. Adorno, Else Frenkel-Brunswik, D. J. Levinson, and R. N. Sanford, *The Authoritarian Personality* (New York, 1950); Edward A. Shils, "Authoritarianism: 'Right' and 'Left'" in *Studies in Scope and Method of "The Authoritarian Personality,"* a symposium edited by Richard Christie and Marie Jahoda (Glencoe, Ill., 1954); and Paul Kechemeti and Nathan Lertes, "Some Psychological Hypotheses on Nazi Germany" in *Journal of Social Psychology,* vol. 27 (May, 1948), pp. 91-117.

The role played by economics in producing Nazism is discussed in W. F. Bruck, *Social and Economic History of Germany from William II to Hitler, 1888-1938* (New York, 1938); Gustav Stolper, *German Economy, 1870-1940: Issues and Trends* (New York, 1940); George W. F. Hallgarten,

"Adolf Hitler and German Heavy Industry, 1931-1933," in *Journal of Economic History,* vol. XII, no. 3 (Summer, 1952), pp. 222-246, and the same author's *Hitler, Reichswehr und Industrie: Zur Geschichte der Jahre 1918-1933* (Frankfurt am Main, 1962); and Gerard Braunthal, "The German Free Trade Unions during the Rise of Nazism," *The Journal of Central European Affairs,* vol. XV (January, 1956), pp. 339-353. For a significant study in military and social history, see G. D. Feldman, *Army, Industry and Labor in Germany, 1914-1918* (Princeton, N.J., 1966). Also useful is F. L. Carsten, *The Reichswehr and Politics, 1919-1933* (London, 1966).

For anti-Semitism and its relationship to Nazism, see the exhaustive bibliography published by the Wiener Library, Catalogue Series No. 3, *German Jewry: Its History, Life and Culture* (London, 1958). Social and psychological aspects of the problem are treated by a group of distinguished psychiatrists, sociologists, and psychologists in Ernst Simmel (ed.), *Anti-Semitism, A Social Disease* (New York, 1946). Other basic books include: Eva Reichman. *Hostages of Civilization: The Social Sources of National Socialist Anti-Semitism* (Boston, 1951); Paul W. Massing, *Rehearsal for Destruction: A Study of Political Anti-Semitism in Imperial Germany* (New York, 1949); and Peter G. J. Pulzer, *The Rise of Political Anti-Semitism in Germany and Austria* (New York, 1964).

The following books show the force of militarism in German history: a monumental multivolume study now in process by Gerhard Ritter, *Staatskunst und Kriegshandwerk: Das Problem des 'Militarismus' in Deutschland* (Munich, 1954-   ); a superb one-volume study, Gordon Craig, *The Politics of the Prussian Army, 1640-1945* (Oxford, 1955); John W. Wheeler-Bennett, *The Nemesis of Power, The German Army in Politics, 1918-1945* (London, 1953); Hans Ernst Fried, *The Guilt of the German Army* (New York, 1942); Hans Herzfeld, "Militarism in Modern German History" in Hans Kohn (ed.), *German History, Some Recent Views* (New York, 1954); Harold J. Gordon, Jr., *The Reichswehr and the German Re-*

public, 1919-1926 (Princeton, N.J., 1957); Robert G. L. Waite, *Vanguard of Nazism, The Free Corps Movement in Postwar Germany, 1918-1923* (Norton Paperback, New York, 1969); and Thilo Vogelsang, *Reichswehr, Statt und NSDAP: Beitrage zur deutschen Geschichte 1930-1932* (Stuttgart, 1963).

The best discussion of German intellectual history as a factor in the genesis of Nazism is George L. Mosse, *The Crisis of German Ideology: Intellectual Origins of the Third Reich* (New York, 1964). See also the books and articles of Vermeil, previously cited; Rohan D'O. Butler, *The Roots of National Socialism* (London, 1941); Peter Viereck, *Metapolitics, The Roots of the Nazi Mind,* rev. ed. (New York, 1962); Hans Kohn, *The Mind of Germany* (New York, 1958); W. W. Coole and M. F. Potter, *Thus Spake Germany* (London, 1941); and S. D. Stirk, *The Prussian Spirit: A Survey of German Literature and Politics, 1914-1940* (London, 1941). Specialized studies of value include: Klemens von Klemperer, *Germany's New Conservatism: Its History and Dilemma in the Twentieth Century* (Princeton, N. J., 1957); Armin Mohler, *Die Konservative Revolution in Deutschland, 1918-1932* (Stuttgart, 1950); and Fritz Stern, *The Politics of Cultural Despair, A Study in the Rise of the Germanic Ideology* (Berkeley and Los Angeles, Calif., 1951). The distinguished intellectual historian and native German, Peter Gay, has written a brilliant essay, *Weimar Culture: The Outsider as Insider* (New York, 1968).

The growth of the Nazi party is traced in the early but still valuable works of Konrad Heiden, notably, *A History of National Socialism* (New York, 1935). A fuller account, albeit apologetic in tone, is given in Georg Franz-Willing, *Die Hitlerbewegung,* a projected multivolume work of which the first volume, *Der Ursprung, 1919-1922* has appeared (Hamburg, 1962). Also valuable are the detailed and authoritative studies by Reginald Phelps, notably his articles, " 'Before Hitler Came': Thule Society and Germanen Orden" in *The Journal of Modern History,* vol. XXV, no. 3 (September, 1963), pp. 245-261; and "Hitler and the Deutsche Arbeiterpartei" in *American Historical Re-*

view, vol. LXVIII, no. 4. (July, 1963), pp. 974-986. A fascinating memoir which re-creates the atmosphere of Hitler's struggle for power is Kurt G. W. Ludecke, *I Knew Hitler* (New York, 1938). A book which argues Hitler's indebtedness to a Viennese racist pamphleteer is Wilfried Daim, *Der Mann der Hitler die Ideen gab* (Munich, 1958); see also George L. Mosse, "The Mystical Origins of National Socialism" in *Journal of the History of Ideas*, vol. XII (January-March, 1961), pp. 81-96.

The study of Adolf Hitler should begin with Alan Bullock's definitive biography, *Hitler, A Study in Tyranny*, rev. ed. (New York, 1962). Still useful is Konrad Heiden's early, *Der Fuehrer* (Boston, 1944). George H. Stein has collected some valuable impressions of Hitler for the series, "Great Lives Observed" (Spectrum Paperback, New York, 1968). Suggestive psychological insights are given in the perceptive essays of James H. McRandle, *The Track of the Wolf: Essays on National Socialism and Its Leader Adolf Hitler* (Evanston, Ill., 1965). A book that gives many insights into Hitler's youth but must be used with caution is August Kubizek, *The Young Hitler I Knew* (Boston, 1955); it should be compared carefully with Franz Jetzinger's *Hitler's Youth* (London, 1958). For a scholarly account which evaluates earlier studies see Bradford F. Smith, *Adolf Hitler: His Family, Childhood and Youth* (Stanford, Calif., 1967). His last days are best described by H. R. Trevor-Roper, *The Last Days of Hitler* (New York, 1947); Gerhard Boldt, *Die letzten Tage der Reichskanzlei*, 4th ed. (Hamburg, 1947) and Albert Zoller (ed.), *Hitler Privat: Erlebnisbericht seiner Geheimsekretärin* (Dusseldorf, 1949). The official Russian autopsy report on the bodies of Hitler and Eva Braun Hitler is reprinted in Lev Bezymenski, *The Death of Adolf Hitler: Unknown Documents from Soviet Archives* (New York, 1968). An article based on an important interview with one of Hitler's valets who takes exception to some of Bezymenski's conclusions is given in the German magazine, *Der Spiegel*, Number 22 (1965). There is a good bibliographical review article by Andreas Dorpalen, "Hitler

Twelve Years After" in *Review of Politics*, vol. 19 (1957), pp. 486-506.

Hitler must also be studied in his own writings. The most useful edition in English of his autobiographical and propagandistic tract, *Mein Kampf*, is that published by Reynal and Hitchcock (New York, 1939); a second book written in 1928 and only recently discovered has been translated under the title, *Hitler's Secret Book* (New York, 1961). Hitler's speeches have been collected in: Norman H. Baynes (ed.), *The Speeches of Adolf Hitler . . .*, 2 vols. (London and New York, 1942); Gordon W. Prange, *Hitler's Words* (Washington, 1944); and Raoul de Roussy de Sales (ed.), *My New Order* (New York, 1941). Two books record Hitler's conversations: Hermann Rauschning, *The Voice of Destruction* (New York, 1940) gives conversations during the period 1932-1934; and a collection of Hitler's banal observations and interminable—but highly revealing—soliloquies of the war years is given in H. R. Trevor-Roper (ed.), *Hitler's Secret Conversations, 1941-1944* (New York, 1953).

Further insight into Hitler's personality and the nature of the Third Reich may be gained by reading the biographies, auto-biographies, diaries, and speeches of other Nazis such as Goebbels, Göring, Himmler, Röhm, Dietrich, Ludecke, Hoffman, Papen, Hanfstaengl, Alfred Rosenberg, Strasser, and Borman, as well as the memoirs of various generals and admirals. See also Nerin E. Gun, *Eva Braun, Hitler's Mistress* (New York, 1968.) Fascinating studies of Nazi leaders have been made by Douglas M. Kelley, a psychiatrist, *22 Cells in Nuremberg* (New York, 1947); and by the prison psychologist at Nuremberg, G. M. Gilbert, *The Psychology of Dictatorship: Based on an Examination of the Leaders of Nazi Germany* (New York, 1950).

The best brief history of the Third Reich is T. L. Jarman, *The Rise and Fall of Nazi Germany* (New York, 1955). Also valuable, particularly for quotations from primary materials and for description of military and foreign affairs, is William L. Shirer, *The Rise and Fall of the Third Reich* (New York, 1960). Revealing German views, in addition to Hannah Vogt's important book, *The Burden of Guilt: A Short History of Germany, 1914-1945* (New York, 1964), are Hermann Mau and Helmut Krausnick, *German History, 1933-45: An Assessment by German Historians* (London, 1959) and Milton Mayer, *They Thought They were Free: The Germans, 1933-1945* (Chicago, 1954), and account based on case histories of ten Nazis. Various aspects of the period are discussed in essays in *The Third Reich*, edited by Baumont *et al.* An early but still basic analysis from the Marxist point of view is Franz Neumann, *Behemoth: The Structure and Practice of National Socialism* (New York, 1944); see also Frederick L. Schuman, *The Nazi Dictatorship* (New York, 1936). An indispensable work analyzing Hitler's technique in consolidating power is the cooperative study by Karl Dietrich Bracher, Wolfgang Sauer, and Gerhard Schulz, *Die nationalsozialistische Machtergreifung: Studien zur Errichtung des totalitären Herrschaftssystems in Deutschland* (Cologne and Opladen, 1960), an English translation of which is forthcoming. The spirit, tone, and terror of Nazi Germany is recaptured in the superb pictorial history, *Das dritte Reich: seine Geschichte in Texten, Bildern und Dokumenten,* edited by Heinz Huber and Autur Müller, two vols. (Munich, Vienna, Basel, 1964). Valuable selections from original documents, letters, speeches, and essays of the period may be found in two books edited by Léon Poliakov and Joseph Wulf: *Das dritte Reich und seine Diener* (Berlin, 1956) and *Das dritte Reich und seine Denker* (Berlin, 1949).

On the Nazi economic structure, in addition to Stolper and Neumann and Burton H. Klein, *Germany's Economic Preparation for War* (Cambridge, Mass., 1959), see Arthur Schweitzer, *Big Business in the Third Reich* (Bloomington, Ind., 1964). Marxist interpretations are given by Jürgen Kucznski, and M. Wit, *The Economics of Barbarism* (New York, 1942); Jürgen Kucznski, *Germany: Economic and Labor Conditions under Fascism* (New York, 1945); Maxine Sweezey, *The Structure of the Nazi Economy,* (Cambridge, Mass., 1941); and Maurice

Dobb, "Aspects of Nazi Economic Policy" in *Science and Society,* vol. IX (Winter, 1945). pp. 96-103. Two useful studies of Schacht and the German economy are those by Earl R. Beck, *Verdict on Schacht . . .* (Tallahassee, Fla., 1956) and Edward N. Peterson, *Hjalmar Schacht: For and Against Hitler: A Political-Economic Study of Germany, 1923-1945* (Boston, 1954). Alan S. Milward gives an excellent account of the war years, *The German Economy at War* (London, 1965).

On rearmament, foreign affairs, and war, the following works are important: Gerhard Meinck, *Hitler und die deutsche Aufrüstung, 1933-1937* (Wiesbaden, 1959); Gordon A. Craig and Felix Gilbert (eds.), *The Diplomats, 1919-1939* (Princeton, N.J., 1953); Paul Seabury, *The Wilhelmstrasse: A Study of German Diplomats under the Nazi Regime* (Berkeley, Calif., 1954); L. B. Namier, *Diplomatic Prelude, 1938-1939* (London, 1948); G. L. Weinberg, *Germany and the Soviet Union, 1939-1941* (Leiden, 1954); Gustav Hilger and Alfred Meyer, *The Incompatible Allies, German-Soviet Relations, 1918-1941* (New York, 1944); Esmonde M. Robertson, *Hitler's Pre-War Policy and Military Plans, 1933-1939* (London, 1959); John W. Wheeler-Bennett, *Munich: Prologue to Tragedy* (London, 1948) and, a definitive account of the same subject, Boris Gelovsky, *Das Münchener Abkommen von 1938* (Stuttgart, 1958); F. W. Deakin, *The Brutal Friendship: Mussolini, Hitler and the Fall of Italian Fascism* (London, 1962). The most judicious commentary on A. J. P. Taylor's thesis on the causes of World War II may be found in a review article by Robert Spencer of Toronto University, "War Unpremeditated?" in *The Canadian Historica Review,* vol. XLIII, no. 2 (June, 1962). Another penetrating essay critical of Taylor's conclusions is that of T. W. Mason, "Some Origins of the Second World War" in *Past and Present* (Oxford, Number 29, December 1964) pp. 67-87. For military strategy and history, see especially H. R. Trevor-Roper (ed.), *Blitzkrieg to Defeat, Hitler's War Directives, 1939-1945* (New York, 1965); Felix Gilbert (ed.), *Hitler Directs His War: The Secret Records of His Daily Military Con-*

ferences (New York, 1950); *Führer Confer-ences on Matters Dealing with the German Navy* (Washington, 1940); Anthony K. Mar-tiensen, *Hitler and His Admirals* (London, 1948). An early, but still valuable brief sum-mary is given by F. H. Hinsley, *Hitler's Strategy* (Cambridge, Mass., 1951). Earl F. Ziemke, *The German Northern Theater of Operations, 1940-45* (Washington, 1960) provides a thorough analysis. An excellent, readable account of the Western campaigns is Telford Taylor, *The March of Conquest* (New York, 1958). Two different positions with regard to the invasion of England are taken by Walter Ansel, *Hitler Confronts England* (Durham, N.C., 1960) and Ronald Wheatly, *Operation Sea Lion: German Plans for the Invasion of England, 1939-1942* (New York and London, 1958). For helpful ap-praisals of the mass of war memoirs, see H. R. Trevor-Roper, "The Germans Reap-praise the War" in *Foreign Affairs*, vol. 31, no. 2 (January, 1953), pp. 225-237. The interpretations of German generals about the war are given in a book edited by the noted British military historian, B. H. Lid-dell Hart, *The Other Side of the Hill* (Lon-don, 1951). For epic accounts of the war on the Eastern front, see Alexander Werth, *Russia at War, 1941-1945* (New York, 1964) and Alan Clark, *Barbarossa: Russian-German Conflict, 1941-45* (New York, 1965). Hitler and his elite corps are well described in George H. Stein, *The Waffen SS, Hitler's Elite Guard at War, 1939-1945* (Ithaca, N.Y., 1966); Hitler's efforts to establish hegemony over Europe are discussed in survey form in Arnold Toynbee (ed.), *Survey of Interna-tional Affairs: Hitler's Europe* (London, 1955) and in the brilliant, detailed, and in-terpretive work by Alexander Dallin, *Ger-man Rule in Russia, 1941-1945* (New York, 1957). See also Ihor Kamenetsky, *Secret Nazi Plans for Eastern Europe: A Study of Leben-sraum Policies* (New York, 1961). Both the ruthless efficiency and the irrationality of Nazi practices are shown in Robert L. Koehl, *RKVD: German Resettlement and Popula-tion Policy* (Cambridge, Mass., 1957). The story of genocide is told in horrifying detail by Paul Hilberg, *The Destruction of the European Jews* (Chicago, 1961) and by Gerald Reitlinger, *The Final Solution* (Lon-don, 1953).

For graphic accounts of totalitarian terror within Germany, see Edward Crankshaw, *Gestapo, Instrument of Tyranny* (New York, 1956); Gerald Reitlinger, *The SS: Alibi of a Nation, 1922-1945* (New York, 1957); Lord Russell of Liverpool, *The Scourge of the Swastica: A Short History of Nazi War Crimes* (London, 1955); Eugene Kogon, *The Theory and Practice of Hell . . .* (New York, 1951, and in paperback, Berkeley, Calif.); E. K. Bramstedt, *Dictatorship and Political Police, The Technique of Control by Fear* (London, 1945). For a gripping description of life in concentration camps, see the work of a Dutch psychiatrist and survivor, Elie A. Cohen, *Human Behavior in the Concentra-tion Camp* (New York, 1953).

The story of underground opposition to the Nazis is told best in the newly revised account of Hans Rothfels, *The German Op-position to Hitler: An Appraisal* (New York, 1963); another important work is Gerhard Ritter, *The German Resistance: Carl Goer-deler's Struggle Against Tyranny* (New York, 1958). A brief but useful interpretation by the head of the American wartime OSS is Allen W. Dulles, *Germany's Underground* (New York, 1947). A view of the opposition drawn from Nazi police and Gestapo files is seen in Bernhard Vollmer (ed.), *Volksoppo-sition im Polizeistaat: Gestapo und Regier-ungsberichte, 1934-1936* (Stuttgart, 1957). Moving and brief life histories of resistance leaders are given in Annedor Leber (ed.), *Conscience in Revolt: Sixty-four Stories of Resistance in Germany, 1933-1945* (London, 1957). The bomb plot against Hitler is re-counted in Constantine Fitzgibbon, *20 July* (New York, 1956).

Other aspects of the Third Reich are de-scribed in such books as these: George L. Mosse (ed.), *Nazi Culture: Intellectual, Cul-tural and Social Life in the Third Reich* (New York, 1966); Barbara M. Lane, *Archi-tecture and Politics in Germany, 1918-1945* (Cambridge, Mass., 1968); Hellmut Lehmann-Haupt, *Art Under a Dictatorship* (London, 1954); Joseph Wulf, *Die Bildenden Künste im Dritten Reich* (Gütersloh, 1964); Edward Y. Hartshone, *The German Universities and National Socialism* (Cambridge, Mass., 1937); G. F. Kneller, *The Educational Philosophy of National Socialism* (New Haven, Conn., 1941); Joseph Wulf, *Musik im Dritten Reich: Eine Dokumentation* (Gütersloh, 1963); Guilford Kirkpatrick, *Nazi Germany: Its Women and Family Life* (New York, 1938); Gregor Ziemer, *Education for Death: The Making of the Nazi* (New York, 1941); Arthur Frey, *Cross and Swastika: The Ordeal of the German Church* (London, 1938); and A. S. Duncan Jones: *The Struggle for Religious Freedom in Germany* (London, 1939). The most authoritative study of the relationship between the Catholic Church and Hitler is Guenther Lewy, *The Catholic Church and Nazi Germany* (New York, 1964). The most comprehensive account of the relationship between the Nazi state and the Christian churches is J. S. Conway, *The Nazi Persecution of the Churches, 1933-1945* (New York, 1968). The best book on propaganda is Z. A. B. Zeman, *Nazi Propaganda* (London, 1964). Social forces are best studied in two scholarly books: Ralf Dahrendorf, *Society and Democracy in Germany* (New York, 1967) and David Schoenbrunn, *Hitler's Social Revolution: Class and Status in Nazi Germany, 1933-1939* (Anchor Paperback, New York, 1967).

Important published documents include: *Fall of the German Empire, 1914-1918,* 2 vols., edited by Ralph H. Lutz (Stanford, Calif., 1932); *Documents on German Foreign Policy, 1918-1945,* Series C and D, edited by Paul Sweet *et al.* (Washington, 1949-   ); *Axis Rule in Occupied Europe,* a collection of laws, orders, regulations, etc., edited by R. Lemkin (London, 1944); *Documents on British Foreign Policy, 1919-1939,* edited by E. L. Woodward and Rohan Butler, 2nd and 3rd Series (London, 1939). A useful collection, but one to be used with caution because of editing, is *Documents and Materials Relating to the Eve of the Second World War* published by the Ministry of Foreign Affairs of the U.S.S.R., 2 vols. (Moscow, 1948). *Nazi-Soviet Relations, 1939-1941* (Washington, 1948) comprises documents from the German Foreign Office archives published by the Department of State and edited by Raymond J. Sontag and James S. Beddie.

Essential for both foreign and domestic affairs are the various Nuremberg documents prepared for the trials after the war. The complete account of the proceedings of the main trial and the full text of documents presented in evidence have been published as *The Trial of the Major War Criminals before the International Military Tribunal, Proceedings,* vols. I-XXIII (Nuremberg, 1947-49) and *Documents in Evidence,* vols. XXIV-XLII (Nuremberg, 1947-49); these constitute the so-called "Blue Series." Translations of most of the documents used by the American and British prosecutors, together with translations of certain of the defense documents and more important affidavits, have been published in a "Red Series": *Nazi Conspiracy and Aggression,* 8 vols., plus two supplementary vols., A and B (Washington, 1946-48). A verbatim record of the trial proceedings has been published by the British Government: *Trial of German Major War Criminals,* 22 parts (London, 1946-50). All these publications retain the same document numbers used at the trial. Subsequent trials, including that of the Nazi doctors, the Krupp and foreign office cases, etc., have been recorded in the "Green Series": *Trials of War Criminals before the Nuremberg Military Tribunals,* 15 vols. (Washington, 1951-53). For guidance to the mass of material collected for the trials, see *Guide to the Records of the United Nations War Crimes Commission, 1943-1948* (U.N. Archives Reference Guide No. 19, August, 1951).

Indispensable for research into other Nazi documents are the various *Guides to German Records Microfilmed at Alexandria, Va.,* issued by the National Archives. Copies of these *Guides* and copies of the actual microfilms of thousands of captured documents may be obtained from the National Archives, Washington, D.C.